Covenants & Blessings

(Formerly TWO COVENANTS)

ANDREW MURRAY

Whitaker House

PITTSBURGH & COLFAX STREETS, SPRINGDALE, PA. 15144

COVENANTS & BLESSINGS

ISBN: 0-88368-136-6
Printed in the United States of America
Copyright © 1984 by Whitaker House
Cover Photo: William D. McKinney/Shostal Associates

Whitaker House
580 Pittsburgh Street
Springdale, PA 15144

5 6 7 8 9 10 11 12 13 14 / 04 03 02 01 00 99 98 97 96 95

Contents

Introduction

It is often said that the great aim of the preacher should be to translate Scripture truth from its Jewish form into the language and thought of the twentieth century. He should make it intelligible and acceptable to ordinary Christians. It is feared that the experiment will do more harm than good. In the course of the translation, the power of the original message is lost. The scholar who trusts translations will never become a master of the language he wants to learn. A race of Christians will arise who will be strangers to the language of God's Word and the God who spoke it. In the wording of some Scripture translations, much of Scripture truth will be lost. For the true Christian life nothing is as healthy and invigorating as having each man come and study for himself the very words the Holy Spirit has spoken.

One of the words of Scripture which is almost obsolete is the word "Covenant." There was a time when it was the keynote of theology and the basis for the Christian life of strong, holy men. We know how in Scotland it entered deep into the national life and thought. It made mighty men. It made men to whom God and His promise and power were wonderfully real. It still brings strength and purpose to those who will take the trouble to bring all their life under the control of the inspiring assurance that they are living in Covenant with God. He has faithfully sworn to fulfill in them every promise He has given.

This book is a humble attempt to show exactly which blessings God has covenanted to us. It gives His assurance that the Covenant must, can, and will be fulfilled. It also shows how we can approach God and the conditions for receiving the full, continual experience of the Covenant blessings. I am confident that if I can lead anyone to listen to what God has to say about His Covenant and to deal with Him as a Covenant God, it will bring them strength and joy.

Not long ago I received a letter from one of my correspondents with the following passage in it: "I think you will excuse and understand me when I say there is one further note of power I would like to have introduced in your next book on intercession. God has been giving me some direct teaching this winter about the place the New Covenant is to have in intercessory prayer.

"I know you believe in the Covenant and the Covenant rights we have because of it. Have you followed out your views of the Covenant as they bear upon this subject of intercession? Am I wrong in coming to the conclusion that we may come boldly into God's presence and not only ask, but claim a Covenant right through Christ Jesus to all the spiritual searching, cleansing, knowledge, and power promised in the three great Covenant promises?

"If you take the Covenant and speak about it as God enables you to speak, I think that would be the quickest way for the Lord to make His Church wake up to the power He has put in our hands in giving us a Covenant. I would be so glad if you told God's people that *they have a Covenant.*" Though this letter was not the occasion of the writing of the book, and our Covenant rights have been considered in a far wider aspect than their relationship to prayer, I am persuaded that nothing will help us more in our work of intercession than the entrance into what it means to have a Covenant God.

My one great desire has been to ask Christians whether they are really seeking to find out exactly what God wants them to be and is willing to make them. It is only as they want "that the mind of the Lord may be showed them." It is only then that their faith can ever truly see, accept, or enjoy what God calls "His salvation." As long as we expect God to do for us only what we ask or think, we limit Him. When we believe that as high as the heavens are above the earth, His thoughts are above our thoughts, and wait on Him as God to do to us *according to His Word,* we will be prepared to live the truly supernatural, heavenly life the Holy Spirit can work in us—the true Christ life.

May God lead every reader into the secret of His presence and "show him His Covenant."

Andrew Murray

Chapter 1

A COVENANT GOD

"Know therefore that the Lord thy God, he is God, the faithful God, which keepeth covenant and mercy with them that love him and keep his commandments"—Deuteronomy 7:9.

Men know the advantages of making covenants. A covenant has often been of unspeakable value as an end to hatred or uncertainty, as an agreement of services rendered, as an assurance of good quality and honesty, and as a basis for confidence and friendship.

God's Covenant

In His infinite descent to our human weakness and need, God's pledge of faithfulness goes beyond the ways of men. He gives us perfect confidence in Him and the full assurance of all that He, in His infinite riches and power, has promised to do. He has consented to bind Himself by Covenant, as if He could not be trusted. Blessed is the man who truly knows God as his Covenant God and knows what the Covenant promises him. What unwavering confidence of expectation it secures. All its terms will be fulfilled to him. What a claim and hold it gives him on the Covenant-keeping God Himself.

To many who have never thought much about the Covenant, it would mean the transformation of their whole life to have a true, living faith. *The full knowledge of what God wants to do, the assurance that it will be done, and the being drawn to God Himself* in personal surrender makes the Covenant the very gate of heaven. May the Holy Spirit give us some vision of its glory.

When God created man in His image and likeness, it was so that he would have a life as similar to God's as possible. This occurred by God Himself living and working all in man. For this, man was to yield himself in loving dependence to the wonderful glory of being the recipient, bearer, and manifestation of a divine life. The one secret of man's happiness was to be a trustful surrender of his whole being to the willing and the working of God. When sin entered, this relationship to God was destroyed. When man disobeyed, he feared God and fled from Him. He no longer knew, loved, or trusted God.

Getting Man To Believe

Man could not save himself from the power of sin. If his redemption was to be affected, God had to do it all. If God was to do it in harmony with the law of man's nature, man must be brought to desire it, yield to it, and entrust himself to God.

All God wanted man to do was believe in Him. What a man believes, moves and rules his whole being. It enters into him and becomes part of his very life. Salvation could only be by faith. God restored the life man had lost. Man in faith yielded himself to God's work and will.

The first great work of God with man was to get him to believe. This work cost God more care, time, and patience than we can conceive. All the dealings with individual men and with the people of Israel had this one object—to teach men to trust Him. Where He found faith He could do anything. Nothing dishonored and grieved Him so much as unbelief. Unbelief was the root of disobedience and every sin. It made it impossible for God to do His work. The one thing God sought to waken in men by promise, mercy, and judgment was faith.

The main way God's patient grace awakened and strengthened faith was the Covenant. In more than one way God sought to effect this by His Covenant. First of all, His Covenant was always *a revelation of His purposes*. It held out, in definite promise, what God was willing to work in those with whom the Covenant was made. It was a divine pattern of the work God intended to do in their behalf so that they might know what to desire and expect. It was a pattern so their faith could nourish itself with the very things, though as yet unseen, which God was working out.

Then, the Covenant was meant to be *a security and guarantee*. It was to be as simple, plain, and humanlike as the divine glory could make it. The very things which God had promised would be brought to pass and worked out in those with whom He had entered into covenant. Amid all delay, disappointment, and apparent failure of the divine promises, the Covenant was to be the anchor of the soul, pledging the divine truthfulness, faithfulness, and unchangeableness for the certain performance of what had been promised. So the Covenant was, above all, to give man *a hold upon God,* as the Covenant-keeping God. It was to link him to God in expectation and hope. It was to cause him to make God alone the portion and the strength of his soul.

Unbelief Holds Us Back

If we only knew how God wants us to trust Him and how His every promise will be fulfilled for those who do so! If we only knew that it is our unbelief that prevents us from entering into the possession of God's promises. Because of this, God cannot do His mighty works in us, for us, and through us! One of the surest remedies for our unbelief—the divinely chosen cure for it—is the Covenant into which God has entered with us!

The whole dispensation of the Spirit, the whole economy of grace in Christ Jesus, the whole of our spiritual life, and the whole of the health, growth, and strength of the Church has been laid down, provided for, and secured in the New Covenant. It is a great shame that the Covenant and its wonderful promises are so little thought of. Its plea for an abounding, unhesitating confidence in God is so little understood. Its claim to the faithfulness of the Omnipotent God is rarely tested. No wonder the Christian life misses the joy, holiness, and heavenliness which God meant and so clearly promises that it should have.

Take God's Promises

Let us listen to God's Word which calls us to know, worship, and trust our Covenant-keeping God. Maybe we will find what we have been looking for: the deep, full experience of all that God's grace can do in us. In the text Moses says, *"Know therefore that the Lord thy God, He is God, the faithful God, which keepeth covenant and mercy* with them that love Him" (Deuteronomy 7:9). Notice what God says in Isaiah, "The mountains shall depart, and the hills be removed; but My kindness shall not depart from thee, *neither shall the covenant of My peace be removed,* saith the Lord that hath mercy on thee" (Isaiah 54:10). The fulfillment of every Covenant promise is more sure than any mountain. In Jeremiah God speaks of the New Covenant, *"And I will make an everlasting covenant with them, that I will not turn away from them,* to do them good; but I will put My fear in their hearts, that they shall not depart from Me" (Jeremiah 32:40). The Covenant secures that God will not turn from us nor we depart from Him. He undertakes both for Himself and us.

Let us earnestly ask whether the lack in our Christian life, especially in our faith, is due to neglect of the Covenant. We have not worshipped nor trusted the Covenant-keeping God. Our soul has not done what God called us to—"to take hold of His Covenant," "to remember the Covenant." No wonder our faith has failed and comes short of the blessing. God could not fulfill His promises in us.

If we begin to examine the terms of the Covenant as the deed of our inheritance and the riches we are to possess even here on earth, we will be different. If we will think of the certainty of their fulfillment and turn to the God who has promised to do it all for us, our life will be different from what it has been. It can and will be all that God desires to make it.

We Need More Of God

The greatest lack of our faith is that we need more of God. We accept salvation as His gift. We do not know that the main blessing of salvation is to prepare us for and bring us back to *that close fellowship with God* for which we were created. All that God has ever done for His people in making a Covenant was to bring them to Himself and to teach them to trust in Him, delight in Him, and be one with Him. It cannot be otherwise.

If God is the very fountain of goodness and glory, beauty and blessedness, the more we can have of His presence, conform to His will, engage in His service, and have Him ruling and working in us, the happier we will be. Only a true, good Christian life, which brings us nearer to God every day, makes us give up everything to have more of Him. No obedience can be too strict, no dependence too absolute, no submission too complete, no confidence too implicit to a person who is learning to count God its highest good and exceeding joy.

In entering into covenant with us, God's one object is to draw us to Himself. He wants to make us entirely dependent upon Him, to bring us into the right position and attitude so He can fill us with Himself, His love, and His blessedness. Let us study the New Covenant. God is at this moment living and walking with us. Let us go to God with the honest purpose and surrender to know what He wants to be in us, and to have us be to Him. The New Covenant will become one of the windows of heaven through which we see into the face and very heart of God.

Chapter 2

THE TWO COVENANTS: THEIR RELATIONSHIP

"It is written, that Abraham had two sons, the one by a bondmaid, the other by a freewoman. But he who was of the bondmaid was born after the flesh; but he of the freewoman by promise. Which things are an allegory: for these are the two covenants"—Galatians 4:22-24.

There are two covenants: the Old Covenant and the New Covenant. God speaks of this very distinctly in Jeremiah where He says, "Behold, the days come. . .that I will make a new covenant with the house of Israel. . .not according to the covenant that I made with their fathers" (Jeremiah 31:31-32). This is quoted in Hebrews, with the addition: "In that He saith, A new covenant, He hath made the first old" (Hebrews 8:13). Our Lord spoke of the New Covenant in His blood. In His dealings with His people and in working out His great redemption, it has pleased God that there are two Covenants.

Why Two Covenants?

It has pleased Him for good and wise reasons which made it necessary that it should be so. The clearer our insight into the reasons and the divine reasonableness of there being two Covenants and their relationship to each other, the more we can understand what the New Covenant means to us.

The Covenants indicate two stages in God's dealing with man. There are two ways of serving God: an elementary one of preparation and promise; and a more advanced one of fulfillment and possession. As the true excellency of the second is revealed to us, we can spiritually enter into what God has prepared for us. Let us try to understand why there should have been two.

The reason is found in the fact that in all fellowship between God and man, there are two parties. Each of them must have the opportunity to prove what their part is in the Covenant. In the Old Covenant man had the opportunity to prove what He could do. This was done with the aid of all the means of grace God could bestow. That Covenant ended in man proving his own unfaithfulness and failure. In the New Covenant God proves what He can do with man, unfaithful and weak as he is, when He is allowed and trusted *to do all the work*. The Old Covenant was dependent on man's obedience, which he could and did break (Jeremiah 31:32). The New Covenant was one which God has promised will never be broken. *He Himself keeps it and ensures our keeping it, so He*

16

makes it an Everlasting Covenant.

The Problem

Let us look a little deeper into this. The relationship of God to fallen man in Covenant is the same as it was to unfallen man as Creator. What was that relationship? God planned to make man in His own image and likeness. The ultimate glory of God is that He has life in Himself. He is independent of all else and owes what He is to Himself alone. If the image and likeness of God was not to be just a name and man was to be like God in the power to make himself what he was to be, he had to have the power of free will and self-determination.

This free will was the problem God had to solve in man's creation in His image. Man was to be a being made by God, and yet he was to be, as far as could be, self-made like God. In all God's treatment of man these two factors were always to be taken into account. God would always take the initiative and be the source of life to man. Man was always supposed to be the recipient and, at the same time, the disposer of the life God bestowed.

When man fell through sin and God entered into a Covenant of salvation, these two sides of the relationship still had to be kept intact. God would always be the first and man the second. Yet man, made in God's image, would always have the time and opportunity to appropriate or reject what God gave. He had the opportunity to prove how far he

17

could help himself and be self-made. His absolute dependence on God was not to be forced on him. If it was really to be a thing of moral worth and true blessedness, it must be his deliberate, voluntary choice.

This is the reason why there was a first and second covenant. In the first, man's desires and efforts would be fully awakened. He would be given time to prove what his human nature, aided by outward instruction, miracles, and grace, could accomplish. When his hopeless captivity under the power of sin had been discovered, the New Covenant came. In it God revealed how man's true liberty from sin and self, his true nobility and Godlikeness, was to be found in absolute dependence on God. It was found in *God's being and doing all within him*.

In the very nature of things there was no other possible way for God to deal with a being whom He had endowed with the Godlike power of a will. All the weight this reason has in God's dealing with His people as a whole is equally as important in dealing with the individual. The two Covenants represent two stages of God's education of man and of man's seeking after God. The progress and transition from the one to the other is not merely chronological or historical. It is also organic and spiritual.

The Transition

In greater or lesser degree the transition from the Old Covenant to the New Covenant is seen in

18

every member of the body, as well as in the body as a whole. Under the Old Covenant there were men in whom the powers of the coming redemption worked mightily. In the New Covenant there are men in whom the spirit of the Old still makes itself manifest. The New Testament proves, in some of its most important epistles, especially those to the Galatians, Romans, and Hebrews, how it is still possible to be held fast in the bondage of the Old Covenant.

This is the teaching of the passage from which our text is taken. Ishmael and Isaac are both found in Abraham's home. One was born of a slave, the other of a free woman. One was after the flesh and will of man, the other through the promise and power of God. One was to be cast out; the other was to be heir of all.

It was a picture held up to the Galatians of the life they were leading as they trusted the flesh. It made a fair show and yet proved—by their being held captive to sin—to be, not of the free but of the bondwoman. Only through faith in the promise and mighty quickening power of God could any of them be made truly free and stand in the freedom with which Christ has made us free.

We Need The New Covenant Spirit

As we proceed to study the covenants and their blessings in the light of this and other scriptures, we will see how they are the divine revelation of two systems of worship. Each has its spirit or life-principle ruling every man who professes to be a

Christian. We will see how the one great cause of the weakness in so many Christians is that the Old Covenant spirit of bondage still rules their lives. We will see that nothing but spiritual insight, with whole-hearted acceptance and a living experience of all the New Covenant pledges *that God will work in us,* can possibly prepare for walking as God wants us to. This truth of there being two stages in our service of God, two degrees of nearness in our worship, is typified by many things in the Old Covenant worship. Perhaps nowhere is it more clear than in the difference between the Holy Place and the Most Holy Place in the temple, with the veil separating them. The priests could always enter into the former to draw near to God. Yet they could not come too near. The veil kept them at a distance. To enter within the Most Holy Place was death.

Once a year the High Priest could enter as a promise of the time when the veil would be taken away and full access to dwell in God's presence would be given to His people. At Christ's death the veil of the temple was torn, and His blood gives us boldness and power to enter into the Holiest of All. We can live there day by day in the immediate presence of God. It is by the Holy Spirit, who came from that Holiest of All where Christ had entered, that we can have the power to live and walk with the consciousness of God's presence in us. The Holy Spirit is to bring us life and make us one with God.

The types of the two Covenants, the spirit of

bondage and the spirit of liberty were not only in Abraham's home. They also existed in God's home in the temple. The priests did not have the liberty of access into the Father's presence. Two classes of Christians are found not only among the Galatians but also throughout the Church. Some are content with the double life, half flesh and half spirit, half self-effort and half grace. Others are not content and are seeking with their whole heart to know fully what deliverance from sin and the abiding full power for a walk in God's presence is. God help us to be satisfied with nothing less. (See Note A on the Second Blessing.)

Chapter 3

THE FIRST COVENANT

"Now therefore, if ye will obey my voice indeed, and keep my covenant, then ye shall be a peculiar treasure unto me"—Exodus 19:5.

"He declared unto you his covenant, which he commanded you to perform, even ten commandments"—Deuteronomy 4:13.

"If ye. . .keep these judgments. . .the Lord thy God shall keep unto thee the covenant"—Deuteronomy 7:12.

"I will make a new covenant with the house of Israel, and with the house of Judah: not according to the covenant that I made with their fathers. . .which my covenant they brake"—Jeremiah 31:31-32.

We have seen that the reason there are two Covenants is the necessity of giving the divine and the human will their due place in the working out of man's destiny. God always takes the initiative. Man must then have the opportunity to do his part and prove either what he can do or needs to have done for him. The Old Covenant was absolutely indispensable to awaken man's desires, call forth his efforts, deepen the sense of dependence on God, convince of his sin and weakness, and prepare him to feel the need of Christ's salvation. In the language of Paul, "Wherefore the law was our school master to bring us unto Christ" (Galatians 3:24). "We were kept under the law, shut up unto the faith which should afterward be revealed" (Galatians 3:23).

Characteristics Of The Old Covenant

To understand the Old Covenant we must always remember its two great characteristics. First, it was of divine appointment, filled with much true blessing, and *absolutely indispensable* for the working out of God's purposes. Second, it was only provisional and preparatory to something higher and, therefore, *absolutely insufficient* for giving the full salvation man needs if his heart or the heart of God is to be satisfied.

Note the terms of this first Covenant. "*If ye* will obey My voice indeed, and keep My covenant, then ye shall be. . .unto Me an holy nation" (Exodus 19:5,6). Or, as it is expressed in Jeremiah 7:23 and Jeremiah 11:4, "Obey My voice, and I will be your God." Obedience, especially in the book of Deuteronomy, is the condition of blessing. "A blessing, if ye obey" (Deuteronomy 11:27). Some ask how God could make a Covenant which He knew man could not keep.

The answer to this reveals the whole nature and object of the Covenant. All education, divine or human, deals with its pupils on the principle: faithfulness in little things is essential to the attainment of greater things. In taking Israel into His training, God dealt with them as men in whom, with all the ruin sin had brought, there was still a conscience to judge good and evil. There was a heart capable of being stirred to long after God and a will to choose the good—to choose God Himself. Before Christ and His salvation could be revealed, understood, and truly appreciated, these faculties of man had to be stirred and awakened.

The Law

The law took men into its training and sought to make the very best that could be made of them by external instruction. Provision had been made in the law for a symbolical atonement and pardon. In all God's revelation of Himself through priest, prophet, and king, and in His intervention in providence and grace, everything possible was done to touch and win the heart of His people. He did all He could to emphasize the appeal of their self-interest or their gratitude, their fear or their love.

Its work did not lack fruit. Under the law, administered by the grace that always accompanied it, a number of men whose great mark was the fear of God and a desire to walk blameless in all His commandments were trained. Yet as a whole, Scripture represents the Old Covenant as a failure. The law had promised life, but it could not give it (Deuteronomy 4:1, Galatians 3:21).

The real purpose God gave it was the very opposite. He meant it as "a ministration of death." He gave it to convince man of his sin and awaken the confession of his frailty and his need of a New Covenant and a true redemption.

It is in this view that Scripture uses such strong expressions—"By the law is *the knowledge of sin*" (Romans 3:20). "The law saith. . .that *every mouth* may be stopped, and all *the world* may become guilty before God" (Romans 3:19). "The law *worketh wrath*" (Romans 4:15). "The law entered, that the offense might abound" (Romans 5:20). "That sin by the commandment might become *exceeding sinful*" (Romans 7:13). "As many as are of the works of the law are *under the curse*" (Galatians 3:10). "We were kept under the law, shut up unto the faith which should afterwards be revealed" (Galatians 3:23). "Wherefore the law was our schoolmaster to bring us unto Christ, that we might be justified by faith" (Galatians 3:24).

The Work of The Law

The great work of the law was to discover what sin was. Its hatefulness is accursed of God. Its misery works temporal and eternal ruin. Its power binds man in hopeless slavery. The only hope of deliverance is divine intervention.

In studying the Old Covenant we should always keep in mind the twofold aspect under which Scripture represents it. It was God's grace that gave Israel the law and made the law work out its purpose in individual believers and in the people as a whole. The entire Old Covenant was an elementary school of grace to prepare man for the fullness of grace and truth in Christ Jesus. A name is generally given to an object according to its main feature. So the Old Covenant is called a ministration of condemnation and death, not because there was no grace in it, but because the law with its curse was the predominating element.

We find the combination of the two aspects with special clearness in Paul's epistles. He speaks of all who are of the works of the law as under the curse (Galatians 3:10). Then almost immediately, he speaks of the law as being our schoolmaster unto Christ into whose charge we had been given until the time appointed by the Father. The Old Covenant is absolutely indispensable for the preparation it had to do. It was utterly insufficient to work a true and full redemption for us.

Sin Versus Holiness

God teaches us two great lessons by it. The one is the lesson of *Sin*; the other the lesson of *Holiness*.

The Old Covenant attains its object only as it brings men to a sense of their utter sinfulness and hopeless inability to deliver themselves. As long as they have not learned this, no offer of the New Covenant life can lay hold of them. As long as an intense longing for deliverance from sin has not taken place, they will naturally fall back into the power of the law and flesh. The holiness which the

New Covenant offers will terrify rather than attract them. The life in the spirit of bondage appears to allow for sin because obedience is declared to be impossible.

The other is the lesson of holiness. In the New Covenant the Triune God promises to do everything. He undertakes to give and keep the new heart, give His own Spirit in it, and give the will and power to obey and do His will. As the one demand of the first Covenant was the sense of sin, one great demand of the New is faith that the need of holiness created by the discipline of God's law will be met in a divine, supernatural way. The law cannot work out its purpose, except to bring a man to lie guilty and helpless before the holiness of God. There the New finds him and reveals God, in His grace, accepting and making him a partaker of His holiness.

Live A New Covenant Life

This book is written with a very practical purpose. Its object is to help believers know that wonderful New Covenant of grace which God has made with them. It was written to lead them into the living, daily enjoyment of the blessed life which the New Covenant secures for them. The practical lesson taught by the fact that the one special work of the first Covenant, to convince of sin, is just what many Christians need. Without it the New Covenant could not come. At conversion they were convicted of sin by the Holy Spirit. But this mainly referred to the guilt of sin, and, in some degree, to its hatefulness.

A real knowledge of the power of sin and their entire and utter inability to cast it out or work in themselves what is good is what they did not learn at once. Until they have learned this, they cannot fully enter into the blessing of the New Covenant. When a man sees that, as he cannot raise himself from the dead, he cannot make or keep his own soul alive, then he becomes capable of appreciating the New Testament promise. Then he is made willing to wait on God to do all in him.

Do you feel that you are not fully living in the New Covenant and its blessings? Do you feel there is still some of the Old Covenant spirit of bondage in you? Come and let the Old Covenant finish its work in you. Accept its teaching that all your efforts are failures. Just like you were content at conversion to fall down as a condemned, death-deserving sinner, be content now to come before God in the confession that, as His redeemed child, you still feel yourself utterly unable to do and be what He asks of you. Begin to ask whether the New Covenant does not have a provision you have never yet understood for meeting your weakness and giving you the strength to do what is well-pleasing to God. You will find the wonderful answer in the assurance that God, by His Holy Spirit, undertakes to work everything in you.

Chapter 4

THE NEW COVENANT

"But this shall be the covenant that I will make with the house of Israel; After those days, saith the Lord, I will put my law in their inward parts, and write it in their hearts; and will be their God, and they shall be my people. And they shall teach no more every man his neighbour, and every man his brother, saying, Know the Lord: for they shall all know me from the least of them unto the greatest of them saith the Lord: for I will forgive their iniquity, and I will remember their sin no more"—Jeremiah 31:33-34.

Because of the wonderful clearness with which he announces the coming Redeemer, both in His humiliation and suffering and in the glory of the Kingdom He was to establish, Isaiah has often been called the evangelical prophet. Yet it was given to Jeremiah, in the above passage, and to Ezekiel, in the parallel one, to foretell what would actually result from the Redeemer's work. He also describes the essential character of the salvation

He was to effect. God's plan is revealed in words which the New Testament (Hebrews 8) takes as the divinely inspired revelation of what the New Covenant is of which Christ is the Mediator.

The New Covenant Blessings

We are shown what He will do in us to make us prepared and worthy to be the people of which He is the God. Through the entire Old Covenant there was always one problem. Man's heart was not right with God. In the New Covenant the evil is remedied. Its central promise is a heart delighting in God's law and capable of knowing and holding fellowship with Him. Let us observe the fourfold blessing that is mentioned.

1. *"I will put My law in their inward parts, and write it in their hearts."* Let us understand this well. In our inward parts, our hearts, there are no separate chambers where the law can be put while the rest of the heart is given to other things. The heart is a unity. The inward parts and the heart are not like a house which can be filled with things of an entirely different nature from what the walls are made of—void of any living, organic connection. No, the inward part, the heart, is the disposition, love, will, and the life.

Nothing can be put into the heart, especially by God, without entering, taking possession of it, securing its affection, and controlling its whole being. This is what God undertakes to do in the power of His divine life and operation. He breathes the very spirit of His law into and

30

through the whole inward being. "I will put it into their inward parts, and write it in their hearts" (Jeremiah 31:33). At Sinai the tables of the Covenant, with the law written on them, were of stone as a lasting substance.

It is easy to understand what that means. The stone was wholly set apart for this one thing—to carry and show this divine writing. The writing and the stone were inseparably connected. Likewise, the heart in which God gets His way and writes His law in power lives wholly to carry that writing. It is unchangeably identified with it. Thus God can realize His purpose in creation and have His child of one mind and spirit with Himself, delighting in doing His will.

When the Old Covenant with the law written on stone had done its work in the discovering and condemning, the New Covenant would give in its stead a life of obedience and true holiness of heart. The whole of the covenant blessing centers in this—the heart being made right and equipped to know God. "And I will give them *an heart to know Me,* that I am the Lord: and they shall be My people, and I will be their God: for they shall return unto Me *with their whole heart"* (Jeremiah 24:7).

2. *"And I will be their God, and they shall be My people."* Do not take these words lightly. They occur most often in Jeremiah and Ezekiel in connection with the promise of the everlasting Covenant. They express the very highest experience of the Covenant relationship. It is only when His

people learn to love and obey His law, when their heart and life are wholly devoted to Him and His will, that He can be the inconceivable blessing which these words express, *"I will be your God."* All I am and have as God will be yours. I will be to you all you need or wish for in a God. In the fullest meaning of the word, I, the Omnipresent, will be ever-present with you in all My grace and love. I, the Almighty One, will work each moment in you by My mighty power. I, the Thrice Holy One, will reveal My sanctifying life within you. I will be your God.

And ye shall be My people, saved and blessed, ruled, guided, and provided for by Me. You will be known and seen to be the people of the Holy One, the God of glory. Let us give our hearts time to meditate and wait for the Holy Spirit to work in us all that these words mean.

3. *"And they shall teach no more every man his neighbour, and every man his brother, saying, Know the Lord, for they shall all know Me, from the least of them unto the greatest of them, saith the Lord."* Individual, personal fellowship with God, for the weakest and the least, is the wonderful privilege of every member of the New Covenant. Each one will know the Lord. That does not mean the knowledge of the mind which is not the equal privilege of all and in itself may hinder the fellowship more than help it. We will know the Lord with the knowledge which means appropriation and assimilation and which is eternal life.

As the Son knew the Father because He was one

with Him and dwelt in Him, the child of God will receive, by the Holy Spirit, that spiritual illumination which will make God the One he knows best. Thus it will be because he loves Him most and lives in Him. The promise, "They shall be all taught of God," will be fulfilled by the Holy Spirit's teaching (John 6:45). God will speak to each one from His Word what he needs to know.

4. *"For I will forgive their iniquities, and I will remember their sin no more."* The word *for* shows that this is the reason for all that precedes. Because the blood of this New Covenant was of such infinite worth and its Mediator and High Priest in heaven of such divine power, there is promised such a divine blotting out of sin that God cannot remember it. It is this entire blotting out of sin which cleanses and sets us free from its power. Thus God can write His law in our hearts and show Himself in power as our God. By His Spirit He can reveal to us His deep things—the deep mystery of Himself and His love. The atonement and redemption of Jesus Christ brought about without us and for us has removed every obstacle and made it meet for God. It also made us meet so that the law in the heart, the claim on our God, and the knowledge of Him should now be our daily life and our eternal portion.

Here we now have the divine summary of the New Covenant inheritance. The last-named blessing, the pardon of sin, is the root of it all. The second, having God as our God, and the third, the divine teaching, are the fruit. The tree that grows on this root and bears such fruit is what is named first—the law in the heart. (See Note B.)

The Heart

The central demand of the Old Covenant, Obey My voice, and I will be your God, has now been met. With the law written on the heart, He can be our God, and we will be His people. Perfect harmony with God's will and holiness in heart and life is the only thing that can satisfy God's heart or ours. This is what the New Covenant gives in divine power. "I will *give them an heart* to know Me, and they shall be My people, and I will be their God: for they shall return to Me *with their whole heart*" (Jeremiah 24:7). The New Covenant life hinges on the state of the new heart *given by God.*

Why, if all this is meant to be literally and exactly true of God's people, do we see and experience so little of this life? There is only one answer—our unbelief! We have already spoken of the relationship of God and man in creation. Sin destroyed the perfection that God intended in His relationship with man. The New Covenant is meant to make this perfect relationship possible and real again. However, God will not force His law into the heart. He can only fulfill His purpose as the heart is willing and accepts His offer. In the New Covenant all is by faith. Let us turn away from what human wisdom and experience says and ask God to teach us what His Covenant and its blessings mean. If we persevere in this prayer in a humble and teachable spirit, we can certainly count on its promise, "They shall teach no more every man his neighbour. . .Know the Lord, for they shall all know Me." *The teaching of God Himself, by the Holy Spirit, to make us understand what He says in His Word, is our Covenant right.* Let us count on it.

It is only by a God-given faith that we can appropriate these God-given promises. It is only by God-given teaching and inward illumination that we can see their meaning and believe them. When God teaches us the meaning of His promises in a heart yielded to His Holy Spirit, then we can believe and receive them in a power which makes them a reality in our life.

Let God Do The Work

Is it really possible, amid the wear and tear of daily life, to walk in the experience of these blessings? Are they really meant for all God's children? Let us, instead, ask the question, "Is it possible for God to do what He has promised?" One part of the promise we believe—the complete and perfect pardon of sin. Why should we not believe the other part—the law written on the heart and the direct, divine fellowship and teaching?

We have been so accustomed to separating what God has joined together: the objective, outward work of His Son and the subjective, inward work of His Spirit. Therefore, we consider the glory of the New Covenant above the Old to consist chiefly in the redeeming work of Christ for us and not equally in the sanctifying work of the Spirit in us. Because of this ignorance and unbelief of the indwelling of the Holy Spirit as the power through whom God fulfills the New Covenant promises, we do not really expect them to be made true to us.

Let us turn our hearts away from all past experience of failure, *caused by nothing but unbelief.* Let us admit fully and heartily what failure has taught us—the absolute impossibility of even a regenerate man walking in God's law in his own strength at the same time. Then let us turn our hearts quietly and trustfully to our Covenant God. Let us hear *what* He says He will do for us and believe Him. Let us rest on His unchangeable faithfulness, the surety of the Covenant, and on His Almighty power and the Holy Spirit working in us. Let us give ourselves to Him as our God. He will prove that what He has done for us in Christ is no more wonderful than what He will do in us every day by the Spirit of Christ.

Chapter 5

THE TWO COVENANTS—IN CHRISTIAN EXPERIENCE

"These (women) are the two covenants; the one from the mount Sinai, which gendereth to bondage, which is Agar. For this Agar answereth to Jerusalem which now is, and is in bondage with her children. But the Jerusalem which is above is free, which is the mother of us all. . . .So then, brethren, we are not children of the bondwoman, but of the free. Stand fast therefore in the liberty wherewith Christ hath made us free, and be not entangled again with the yoke of bondage"—Galatians 4:24-31; 5:1.

The house of Abraham was the Church of God at that time. The division in his house—one son, born after the flesh, the other after the promise— was a divinely ordained manifestation of the division that would exist down through the ages. This division was between the children of the bondwoman, who served God in the spirit of bondage, and those who were children of the free, who served Him in the Spirit of His Son. The passage teaches us what the whole epistle confirms. The Galatians had become entangled in a yoke of bondage and were not standing fast in the freedom with which Christ brings.

Instead of living in the New Covenant—the Jerusalem which is from above and the liberty which the Holy Spirit gives—their whole walk proved that, though Christians, they were of the Old Covenant which brings forth children of bondage. The passage teaches us the great truth which is of the utmost consequence for us to understand thoroughly. A man with a measure of the knowledge and experience of the grace of God may prove, by a legal spirit, that he is yet under the Old Covenant. It will also show us, with wonderful clearness, the characteristics of the absence of the true New Covenant life.

The Old Contrasted With The New

A careful study of the epistle shows us that the difference between the two Covenants is seen in three things. *The law and its works* is contrasted with the hearing of faith. *The flesh and its religion* is contrasted with the flesh crucified. *The inability to do good* is contrasted with a walk in the liberty and power of the Spirit. May the Holy Spirit reveal this twofold life to us.

The Law

We find the first contrast in Paul's words, "Received ye the Spirit by the works of the law, or by the hearing of faith?" (Galatians 3:2). These

Galatians had certainly been born into the New Covenant. They had received the Holy Spirit. But, they had been led away by Jewish teachers, and, though they had been justified by faith, they were seeking to be sanctified by works. They were looking for the maintenance and growth of their Christian life in the observance of the law. They had not understood that the progress of the divine life is by faith alone. Day by day it receives its strength from Christ alone. In Jesus Christ nothing avails but faith working by love.

Almost every believer makes the same mistake as the Galatian Christians. Very few learn at conversion that it is only by faith that we stand, walk, and live. They have no idea of the meaning of Paul's teaching about being dead to the law and freed from the law—the freedom with which Christ makes us free. "If ye be led of the Spirit ye are not under the law" (Galatians 5:18).

Regarding the law as a divine ordinance for our direction, they consider themselves prepared and equipped by conversion to take up the fulfillment of the law as a natural duty. They do not know that in the New Covenant the law written in the heart needs an unceasing faith in a divine power to enable them by a divine power to keep it. They cannot understand that it is not to the law but to a Living Person that we are now bound. Our obedience and holiness are only possible by the unceasing faith in His power ever-working in us. It is only when this is seen that we are truly prepared to live in the New Covenant.

The Flesh

The second word that reveals the Old Covenant spirit is the word "flesh." Its contrast is the flesh crucified. Paul asks, "Are ye so foolish? Having begun in the Spirit, are ye now made perfect by the flesh?" (Galatians 3:3). Flesh means our sinful, human nature. At his conversion the Christian generally has no conception of the terrible evil of his nature and the subtlety with which it offers itself to take part in the service of God.

Man's nature may be very willing and diligent in God's service for a time. It may devise numerous observances for making His worship pleasing and attractive. Yet this may only be what Paul calls "making a fair show in the flesh," "glorying in the flesh," in man's will and man's efforts. The power of the religious flesh is one of the great marks of the Old Covenant religion. It misses the deep humility and spirituality of the true worship of God—a heart and life entirely dependent upon Him.

The proof that our faith is very much like that of the religious flesh is that the sinful flesh will flourish along with it. It was so with the Galatians. While they were making a fair show in the flesh and glorying in it, their daily life was full of bitterness, envy, hatred, and other sins. They were biting and devouring one another. Religious flesh and sinful flesh are one. No wonder that, in many Christians, temper, selfishness, and worldliness are so often found side by side. The faith of the flesh cannot conquer sin.

What a contrast to the faith of the New Covenant! What is the place of the flesh there? "They that are Christ's have *crucified the flesh,*with the affections and lusts" (Galatians 5:24). Scripture speaks of the will of the flesh, the mind of the flesh, and the lust of the flesh. The true believer has seen that this is to be condemned and crucified in Christ. He has given it over to the death. He accepts the cross, with its bearing of the curse and its redemption from it, as his entrance into life. He also glories in it as his only power to daily overcome the flesh and the world.

"I am crucified with Christ" (Galatians 2:20). "But God forbid that I should glory, save in the cross of our Lord Jesus Christ, by whom the world is crucified unto me, and I unto the world" (Galatians 6:14). Just as nothing less than Christ's death was needed to inaugurate the New Covenant and the resurrection life, there is no entrance into true New Covenant life except by partaking of that death.

The Inability To Do Good

"Fallen from grace." This is a third word that describes the condition of the Galatians. Paul is not speaking of a final falling away here, for he still addresses them as Christians. But, they have wandered from that walk in the way of enabling and sanctifying grace where a Christian gains victory over sin.

As long as grace is principally connected with

pardon and the entrance to the Christian life, the flesh is the only power in which to serve and work. But, when we know what exceeding abundance of grace has been provided and how God "is able to make all grace abound toward you; that ye. . .may abound to every good work," we know that it is by faith and grace that we stand a single moment or take a single step (2 Corinthians 9:8).

The contrast to this life of failure is found in the one word, "the Spirit." "If ye be led of the Spirit, ye are not under the law" (Galatians 5:18), with its demand on your own strength. "Walk in the Spirit, and ye shall not"—a definite promise—"fulfill the lust of the flesh" (Galatians 5:16). The Spirit gives liberty from the law, the flesh, and from sin. "The fruit of the Spirit is love, peace, joy" (Galatians 5:22). The Spirit is the center and the sum of the New Covenant promise, "I will put *My Spirit* within you, and *cause* you to walk in My statutes, and *ye shall keep* My judgments" (Ezekiel 36:27). He is the power of the supernatural life of true obedience and holiness.

What course would the Galatians have taken if they had accepted this teaching of St. Paul? As they heard his question, "Now, after that ye have known God, how turn ye again to the weak and beggarly elements, whereunto ye desire again to be in bondage?" (Galatians 4:9) they understood that there was only one course. Nothing else could help them except to turn back to the path they had left. At the point where they had left it, they could enter again.

This turning away from the Old Covenant legal spirit and renewing the surrender to the Mediator of the New Covenant could be the act of a moment—one single step. As the light of the New Covenant promise dawns upon you and you see how Christ is all—faith all, the Holy Spirit in the heart all, and the faithfulness of a Covenant-keeping God all in all—you will feel you have one thing to do. In utter weakness you must yield yourself to God. In simple faith you must count on Him to perform what He has spoken. In Christian experience there may still be the Old Covenant life of bondage and failure. In Christian experience there may be a life that gives in entirely to the New Covenant grace and spirit. When a Christian receives the true vision of what the New Covenant means, a faith that rests entirely on the Mediator of the New Covenant can immediately enter the life which the Covenant secures.

The Reason For Failure

I beg all believers, who sincerely want to know what the grace of God can work in them, to carefully study the question of whether the reason for our failure is our being in bondage to the Old Covenant. They should also study whether a clear insight into the possibility of an entire change in our relationship to God is not what is needed to give us the help we seek. We may be seeking growth in a more diligent use of the means of grace and a more earnest striving to live in accordance with God's will and yet fail.

43

The reason is that there is a secret root of evil which must be removed. That root is the spirit of bondage, the legal spirit of self-effort, which hinders the humble faith that knows that God will work out all and yields to Him to do it. That spirit can be found amid great zeal for God's service and very earnest prayer for His grace. It does not enjoy the rest of faith and cannot overcome sin because it does not stand in the liberty with which Christ has made us free. It does not know that where the Spirit of the Lord is there is liberty.

There the soul can say, "The law of the Spirit of life in Christ Jesus *hath made me free* from the law of sin and death" (Romans 8:2). Once we admit that are there failings in our life and also that something radically wrong can be changed, we will turn with new interest, deeper confession of ignorance and weakness, and hope that looks to God alone for teaching and strength. We will find that in the New Covenant there is an actual provision for every need.

Chapter 6

THE EVERLASTING COVENANT

"They shall be my people, and I will be their God. . . .And I will make an everlasting covenant with them, that I will not turn away from them, to do them good; but I will put my fear in their hearts, that they shall not depart from me"—Jeremiah 32:38,40.

"A new heart also will I give you, and a new spirit will I put within you: and I will take away the stony heart out of your flesh, and I will give you an heart of flesh. And I will put my Spirit within you, and cause you to walk in my statutes, and ye shall keep my judgments, and do them. . .Moreover, I will make a covenant of peace with them; it shall be an everlasting covenant with them"—Ezekiel 36:26,27; 37:26.

We have already heard about the institution of the New Covenant. Listen to further teaching we have concerning it in Jeremiah and Ezekiel where God speaks of it as an everlasting Covenant.

In every covenant there are two parties. The very foundation of a covenant rests on the thought

45

that each party is to be faithful to the part it has undertaken to perform. Unfaithfulness on either side breaks the covenant.

It was so with the Old Covenant. God had said to Israel, *"Obey My voice, and I will be your God"* (Jeremiah 6:23; 11:4). These simple words contained the whole Covenant. When Israel disobeyed, the Covenant was broken. The question of Israel being able or unable to obey was not taken into consideration. Disobedience forfeited the privileges of the Covenant.

Securing Obedience

If a new and better covenant were to be made, this was the one thing to be provided for. No New Covenant could be beneficial unless provision were made for securing obedience. There must be obedience. God as Creator could never take His creatures into His favor and fellowship unless they obeyed Him. That would have been an impossibility. If the New Covenant is to be an everlasting Covenant, never to be broken, it must make sufficient provision for securing the obedience of the Covenant people.

This is the glory of the New Covenant, that this provision has been made. The New Covenant, which no human thought could have devised or implemented, was an undertaking in which God's infinite condescension, power, and faithfulness were wonderfully exhibited. By a supernatural mystery of divine wisdom and grace, the New Covenant provides a guarantee not only for God's faithfulness, *but for man's, too!* There is no other way than by God Himself undertaking to secure man's part as well as His own. Try to understand this.

Because this essential part of the New Covenant so exceeds and confounds all human thoughts of what a covenant means, Christians throughout history have been unable to see and believe what the New Covenant really means. They thought that human unfaithfulness was a factor to be permanently dealt with as something utterly unconquerable and incurable. The possibility of a life of obedience, with the witness from within of a good conscience and of God's pleasure above, was not to be expected. Therefore, they sought to stir the mind to its utmost by arguments and motives. They never realized how the Holy Spirit is to be the unceasing, universal, all-sufficient worker of everything that has to be done by the Christian. Let us earnestly ask God to reveal, by the Holy Spirit, the wonderful life of the New Covenant that He has prepared for those who love Him. All depends upon our knowledge of what God will work in us.

God's Covenant Promises

Listen to what God says in Jeremiah about the two parts of His everlasting Covenant shortly after He had announced the New Covenant and further explained it. The central thought of that, *that the heart is to be put right,* is repeated and confirmed here. "I will make an everlasting covenant with them, *that I will not turn away from them, to do them good"* (Jeremiah 32:40). That is, God will be unchangeably faithful. He will not turn from us. "But *I will put My fear into their heart, that they shall not depart from Me"* (Jeremiah 32:40). This is the second half; Israel will be unchangeably faithful, too. Because God will so put His fear in their heart, they will not depart from Him. *As little as God will turn from them, will they depart from Him!* As faithfully as He undertakes for the fulfillment of His part, He will undertake for the fulfillment of their part, that they will not depart from Him!

Listen to God's Word in Ezekiel, in regard to one of the terms of His Covenant of peace, His everlasting Covenant. "And I will put My spirit within you, and *cause you to walk in My statutes,* and *ye shall keep* My judgments, and do them" (Ezekiel 36:27). In the Old Covenant we have nothing of this sort. On the contrary, from the story of the golden calf and the breaking of the Tables of the Covenant onward you have the sad fact of continual departure from God.

We find God longing for what He would so willingly have seen, but it was not to be found. "O that there were such an heart in them, that they would fear Me, and keep all My commandments always" (Deuteronomy 5:29). We find throughout the book of Deuteronomy that Moses distinctly prophesies their forsaking of God with the terrible curses and dispersion that would come upon them.

It is only at the close of Moses' threatenings that

he gives the promise of the new time that would come. "And the Lord thy God will circumcise thine heart, and the heart of thy seed, to love the Lord thy God with all thine heart, and with all thy soul, that thou mayest live" (Deuteronomy 30:6). The entire Old Covenant was dependent on man's faithfulness. "The Lord thy God *keepeth covenant* and mercy with them *that keep* His commandments" (Deuteronomy 7:9). God's keeping the Covenant would mean very little if man did not keep it. Nothing could help man until the *"If ye shall diligently keep"* (Deuteronomy 11:22) of the law was replaced by the word of promise, "I will put My Spirit within you, and *ye shall keep* My judgments, and do them" (Ezekiel 36:27).

The Heart Of Man

The one supreme difference of the New Covenant for which the Mediator, the Blood, and the Spirit were given was a heart filled with His fear and love, cleaving to Him and not departing from Him. The one fruit God sought and engaged to bring forth was this: a heart in which His Spirit and His law dwells and a heart that delights to do His will.

Here is the innermost secret of the New Covenant. It deals with the heart of man in a way of divine power. It not only appeals to the heart by every motive of fear, love, duty, or gratitude, like the law did, but it also reveals God Himself cleansing our heart and making it new, changing it from a stony heart into a heart of flesh, and making it a

49

tender, living, loving heart. He puts His Spirit within it and, by His almighty power and love, breathes and works in it to make the promise true, *"I will cause you* to walk in My statutes, and *ye shall keep* My judgments"* (Ezekiel 36:27). A heart in perfect harmony with Himself, a life and walk in His way, this is what God has engaged in Covenant to work in us. He undertakes for our part in the Covenant as much as for His own.

This is nothing but the restoration of the original relationship between God and the man He had made in His likeness. Man was on earth to be the very image of God because God was to live and work all in him. Man was to find his glory and blessedness in owing all to God. This is the exceeding glory of the New Covenant: that, by the Holy Spirit, God could again be the indwelling life of His people. Thus He can make the promise a reality, "I will cause you to walk in My statutes."

With God's presence secured to us, His "fear put into our heart" by His Spirit, and our heart thus responding to His holy presence, we can and will walk in His statutes and keep His judgments.

Don't Limit God

Brethren, Israel's great sin under the Old Covenant by which they greatly grieved Him was this: "they limited the Holy One of Israel" (Psalm 78:41). Under the New Covenant there is still the danger of this sin. *It makes it impossible for God to fulfill His promises.* Above everything, let us seek the Holy Spirit teaching to show us exactly what God has established the New Covenant for. In this way we will honor Him by believing all that His love has prepared for us.

If we ask for the cause of the unbelief that prevents the fulfillment of the promise, we will find that we do not have to look far. In most cases, it is the lack of desire for the promised blessing. The intensity of their desire for their needed healing made all who came to Jesus ready and glad to believe in His Word. Where the law has done its full work and where the actual desire to be freed from every sin is strong and masters the heart, the presence of the New Covenant, when it is really understood, comes like bread to a starving man.

The subtle belief that it is impossible to be kept from sinning destroys the power of accepting the promises of the everlasting Testament promise. God's Word, "I will put My fear in their heart, that *they shall not* depart from Me" and "I will put My Spirit within you, and *ye shall* keep My judgment," is understood in some feeble sense— according to our experience and not according to what the Word and God means. The soul settles into a despair of self-contentment that says it can never be otherwise. It makes true conviction for sin impossible.

Let me speak to every reader who would gladly believe all that God says. Cherish every whisper of the conscience and the Spirit that convicts of sin. Whatever it is, a hasty temper, a sharp word, an unloving or impatient thought, anything of selfishness or self-will, cherish that which condemns it in you as part of the schooling that is to bring you to Christ and the full possession of His salvation. The New Covenant is meant to meet the need for the power of not sinning which the Old could not give. Come with that need. It will prepare and open your heart for all the everlasting Covenant frees you from.

Chapter 7

THE NEW COVENANT: A MINISTRATION
OF THE SPIRIT

*"Ye are manifestly declared to be the epistle of
Christ, ministered by us, written not with ink,
but with the Spirit of the living God; not on
tables of stone, but in fleshly tables of the
heart. . . .Our sufficiency is of God; who also
hath made us able ministers of the new testament; not of the letter, but of the Spirit: for the
letter killeth, but the Spirit giveth life. But if the
ministration of death, written and engraven in
stones, was glorious. . . .How shall not the ministration of the Spirit be rather glorious? For if
the ministration of condemnation be glory,
much rather doth the ministration of righteousness exceed in glory"*—2 Corinthians 3:3,6-10.

In this wonderful chapter Paul reminds the
Corinthians of the chief characteristics of his ministry among them. He contrasts it as a ministry of
the New Covenant and the whole dispensation of
which it is part with that of the Old. The Old was
written on stone; the New on the heart. The Old

could be written in ink and was in the letter that killed. The New, of the Spirit, makes alive. The Old was a ministration of condemnation and death. The New was of righteousness and life. The Old had its glory, for it was of divine appointment and brought its divine blessing. But, it was a glory that passed away.

With the Old there was the veil on the heart. In the New, the veil is taken away from the face and the heart. The Spirit of the Lord gives liberty. Reflecting with unveiled face the glory of the Lord, we are changed from glory to glory, into the same image by the Spirit of the Lord. The glory that excels proved its power in this. It not only marked the dispensation on its divine side but exerted its power in the heart and life of its subjects, so that it was seen in them, as they were changed by the Spirit into Christ's image, from glory to glory.

Think for a moment about the contrast. The Old Covenant was of the letter that killed. The law came with its literal instruction. It sought by the knowledge it gave of God's will to appeal to man's fear, love, and his natural powers of mind, conscience, and will. It spoke to him as if he could obey, so that it could convince him of what he did not know: that he could not obey. So it fulfilled its mission. "The commandment which was unto life, this I found to be unto death."

The Work Of The Spirit

In the New, however, everything was different.

54

Instead of the letter, the Spirit that gives life breathes the very life of God into us. Instead of a law graven in stone, the law written in the heart is worked into the heart's affection and powers making it one with them. Instead of the vain attempt to work from without inward, the Spirit and the law are put into the inward parts to work outward in life and walk.

This passage brings the distinctive blessing of the New Covenant into view. In working out our salvation God bestowed two wonderful gifts on us. We read, *"God sent forth His Son. . .to redeem them that were under the law, that we might receive the adoption of sons. And because ye are sons, God hath sent forth the Spirit of His Son into your hearts, crying, Abba, Father"* (Galatians 4:4-6). Here we have the two parts of God's work in salvation.

The more objective part He did so that we might become His children. He sent forth His Son. The more subjective part He did so that we might live like His children. He sent forth the Spirit of His Son into our hearts. In the former we have the external manifestation of the work of redemption. In the other, we have its inward appropriation, the former for the sake of the latter. These two halves form one great whole and cannot be separated.

In the promises of the New Covenant, found in Jeremiah and Ezekiel as well as in our text and many other passages of Scripture, it is evident that God's great object in salvation is to acquire possession of the heart. The heart is the real life. With the heart a man loves, wills, and acts. The heart makes the man. God made man's heart for His own dwelling so that in it He might reveal His love and glory. God sent Christ to accomplish a redemption by which man's heart could be won back to Him. Nothing but that could satisfy God.

That is what is accomplished when the Holy Spirit makes the heart of His child what it should be. The whole work of Christ's redemption—His atonement, victory, exaltation, intercession, and His glory at the right hand of God—are only preparatory to the major triumph of His grace: the renewal of the heart to be the temple of God. Through Christ, God gives the Holy Spirit to glorify Him in the heart, by working there all that He has done and is doing for the soul.

New Covenant Promises

In a great deal of our spiritual teaching, the fear that we detract from Christ's honor is taught as the reason for giving His work for us, on the cross or in heaven, a greater prominence than His work in our heart by the Holy Spirit. The result has been that the indwelling of the Holy Spirit and His mighty work as the life of the heart are known or experienced very little. If we look carefully at what the New Covenant promises mean, we will see how the "sending forth of the Spirit of His Son into our hearts" is the consummation and crown of Christ's redeeming work. Let us think of what these promises imply.

In the Old Covenant, man failed in what he had

to do. In the New, God does everything in him. The Old could only convict of sin. The New puts it away and cleanses the heart from its filthiness. In the Old it was the heart that was wrong. For the New, a new heart is provided into which God puts His fear, His law, and His love. The Old demanded but failed to secure obedience. In the New, God causes us to walk in His judgments.

The New prepares man for true holiness. It is a true fulfillment of the law of loving God with the whole heart and our neighbors as ourselves. It is a walk truly pleasing to God. The New changes a man from glory to glory after the image of Christ, all because the Spirit of God's Son is given to the heart. The Old gave no power. In the New all is by the Spirit, the mighty power of God. As complete as the reign and power of Christ on the throne of heaven is, so is His dominion on the throne of the heart by His Holy Spirit given to us. (See Note C.)

As we bring all these traits of the New Covenant life together and look at the heart of God's child as the object of this mighty redemption, we will begin to understand what it guarantees us and what we are to expect from our Covenant God. We will see what the glory of the ministration of the Spirit consists of. God can fill our hearts with His love and make it His abode.

We Need The Spirit

We are accustomed to saying that the worth of the Son of God, who came to die for us, is the measure of the worth of the soul in God's sight

57

and the greatness of the work that had to be done to save it. Let us also see that the divine glory of the Holy Spirit is the measure of God's longing to have our heart wholly for Himself, the glory of the work that is to be formed within us, and of the power by which that work will be accomplished.

We will see that the glory of the ministration of the Spirit is no other than the glory of the Lord. This is true not only in heaven but also here on earth, resting on us, dwelling in us, and changing us into the same image from glory to glory. The inconceivable glory of our exalted Lord in heaven has its counterpart here on earth in the exceeding glory of the Holy Spirit. He glorifies Him in us and lays His glory on us as He changes us into His likeness.

The New Covenant has no power to save and bless except as it is a ministration of the Spirit. That Spirit works in lesser or greater degree as He is neglected and grieved or yielded to and trusted. Let us honor Him and give Him His place as the Spirit of the New Covenant by expecting and accepting all He waits to do for us. He is the great gift of the Covenant. His coming from heaven was the proof that the Mediator of the Covenant was on the throne in glory and could now make us partakers of the heavenly life.

He is the only teacher of what the Covenant means. Dwelling in our heart, He awakens the thought and desire for what God has prepared for us.

He is the Spirit of faith who enables us to

believe the otherwise incomprehensible blessing and power in which the New Covenant works and claims it as our own.

He is the Spirit of grace and of power by whom the obedience of the Covenant and the fellowship with God can be maintained without interruption.

He is the Possessor, Bearer, and Communicator of all the Covenant promises. He is the Revealer and Glorifier of Jesus, its Mediator and Surety.

To fully believe in the Holy Spirit as the present, abiding, and all-comprehending gift of the New Covenant has been an entrance into its fullness of blessing to many people.

Child of God, begin at once to give the Holy Spirit the place in your life that He has in God's plan. Be still before God and believe that He is in you. Ask the Father to work in you through Him. Regard yourself, spirit as well as body, with holy reverence as His temple. Let the consciousness of His holy presence and working fill you with holy calm and fear. Be sure that all God calls you to be, Christ through His Spirit will work in you.

Chapter 8

THE TWO COVENANTS: THE TRANSITION

"Now the God of peace, that brought again from the dead our Lord Jesus that great Shepherd of the sheep, through the blood of the everlasting covenant, make you perfect in every good work to do his will, working in you that which is well-pleasing in his sight, through Jesus Christ" — Hebrews 13:20-21.

The transition from the Old Covenant to the New was not slow or gradual, but by a tremendous crisis. Nothing less than the death of Christ could close the Old. Nothing less than His resurrection from the dead, through the blood of the everlasting Covenant, could open the New. The path of preparation which led to the crisis was long and slow. The rending of the veil that symbolized the end of the old worship was the work of a moment. By His death, once and for all, Christ's work as fulfiller of law and prophets was finished forever. By His resurrection in the power of an endless life, the Covenant of Life was ushered in.

Characteristics Of The Covenants

These events have an infinite significance in revealing the character of the Covenants they are related to. The death of Christ shows the true nature of the Old Covenant. It is elsewhere called "a ministration of death" (2 Corinthians 3:7). It brought nothing but death. It ended in death. Only by death could the life that had been lived under it be brought to an end. The New was to be a Covenant of Life. It had its birth in the omnipotent resurrection power that brought Christ from the dead.

Its one mark and blessing is that all it gives comes not only as a promise, but as an experience in the power of an endless life. The death reveals the utter *ineffectiveness* and *insufficiency* of the Old. The life brings near and imparts to us forever all that the New has to offer. An insight into the completeness of the transition, as seen in Christ, prepares us for understanding the reality of the change in our life. "Like as Christ was raised up from the dead by the glory of the Father, even so we also should walk in newness of life" (Romans 6:4).

The complete difference between the life in the Old and the New is remarkably illustrated in Hebrews 9:16. After having said that a death for the redemption of transgression had to take place before the New Covenant could be established, the writer adds, "Where a testament is, there must also of necessity be the death of the testator"

(Hebrews 9:16). Before any heir can obtain the legacy, its first owner, the testator, must have died. The old proprietorship, the old life, must disappear entirely before the new heir, the new life, can enter into the inheritance. Nothing but death can work the transference of the property. It is also true with Christ, the Old and the New Covenant life, and our own deliverance from the Old and our entrance into the New. Having been made dead to the law by the body of Christ, we have been discharged from the law. We have died to that which bound us—here is the completeness of the deliverance from Christ's side. "So that we serve"—here is the completeness of the change in our experience—"in newness of the spirit, and not in oldness of the letter."

A Ministration Of Death

The transition, if it is to be real and whole, must take place by a death. As it is with Christ the Mediator of the Covenant, so it must also be with His people, the heirs of the Covenant. In Him we are dead to sin and the law. Just as Adam died to God and we inherit a nature dead in sin to God and His Kingdom, so in Christ we died to sin and inherit a nature dead to sin and its dominion. When the Holy Spirit reveals and makes real this death to sin and the law as the one condition of a life yielded to God, the transition from the Old to the New Covenant can be fully realized in us.

The Old was meant to be a "ministration of death." Until it has completely done its work in us, there is no complete discharge from its power. Man must see that self is incurably evil and must die. He must give self utterly to death as he sinks before God in utter weakness and surrenders to His working. He must consent to death with Christ on the cross and in faith accept it as his only deliverance. He alone is prepared to be led by the Holy Spirit into the full enjoyment of the New Covenant life. He will learn to understand how completely death makes an end to all self-effort. He will discover how, as he lives in Christ to God, everything from now on is to be the work of God Himself.

See how beautifully our text brings this truth out. Just as much as Christ's resurrection out of death was the work of God Himself, our life is to be entirely God's own work, too. The experience of what the New Covenant life is to bring in us should be as direct and wonderful as Christ's transition from death to life.

Notice the subject of the two verses. In verse 20 we have what God *has done* in raising Christ from the dead. In verse 21 we have what God *is to do in us,* working in us what is pleasing to Him. "Now the God of peace, brought again from the dead our Lord Jesus, that great Shepherd of the sheep. . . make you perfect in every good work to do His will, working in you that which is well-pleasing in His sight, through Jesus Christ" (Hebrews 13:20-21). We have the name of our Lord Jesus mentioned twice. In the first case it refers to what God has done to Christ for us, raising Him. In the second case it refers to what God is doing through

Christ in us, working His pleasure in us.

From Death To Life

Because it is the same God continuing in us the work He began in Christ, it is in us just what it was in Christ. In Christ's death we see Him in utter submission allowing and counting upon God to work all and give Him life. God worked out the wonderful transition. In us we see the same thing. It is only as we also give ourselves to that death, cease entirely from self and its works, and lie as in the grave waiting for God to work all, that the God of resurrection life can work in us all His good pleasure.

It was "through the blood of the everlasting Covenant," with its atonement for sin and its destruction of sin's power, that God effected that resurrection. It is through that same blood that we are redeemed, freed from the power of sin, and made partakers of Christ's resurrection life. The more we study the New Covenant, the more we will see that its one aim is to restore man, out of the Fall, to the life in God for which he was created. First, it does this by delivering him from the power of sin in Christ's death. Then it takes possession of his heart and his life for God to work all in him by the Holy Spirit. The whole argument of the epistle to the Hebrews concerning the Old and New Covenants is summed up here in these concluding verses. Just as He raised Christ from the dead, the God of the everlasting Covenant can and will now make you perfect in every good thing to do His will. He will work in you that which is well-pleasing in His sight through Jesus Christ.

Your doing His will is the object of creation and redemption. God's working all in you is what redemption has made possible. The Old Covenant of law, effort, and failure has ended in condemnation and death. The New Covenant is coming to give, in all whom the law has slain and brought to bow in their utter failure, the law written on the heart, the Spirit dwelling there, and God working all, both to will and to do through Jesus Christ.

God Working All In All

We need a divine revelation that the transition from Christ's death in its humility to His life in God's power is the image, pledge, and power of our transition out of the Old Covenant into the New, with God working in us all in all!

The transition from Old to New, as effected in Christ, was sudden. Is it also in the believer? Not always. It depends upon a revelation in us. There have been cases in which a believer, sighing and struggling against the yoke of bondage, has in one moment seen the complete salvation the New Covenant brings to the heart and the inner life through the ministration of the Spirit. By faith he has entered at once into his rest. There have been other cases in which, as gradually as the dawn of day, the light of God has touched the heart. God's offer of entrance into the enjoyment of our New Covenant privileges is always urgent and immediate. Every believer is a child of the New Covenant and heir to all its promises. The death and resurrection of Christ gives him full right to immediate possession. God longs to bring us into the land of promise. Let us not fail because of unbelief.

May God reveal to us the difference between the two lives under the Old and the New. In the resurrection power of the New, God works all in us. In the power of the transition secured for us in death with Christ there is life in Him. May He teach us at once to trust Christ Jesus for a full participation in all that the New Covenant secures.

There may be someone who can hardly believe that such a mighty change in his life is within his reach. Yet he would gladly know what he is to do if there is to be any hope of his attaining it. I have just said, the death of the testator gives the heir immediate right to the inheritance. Yet the heir, if he is a minor, does not enter into the possession. A term of years ends the stage of minority on earth, and he is no longer under guardians.

In the spiritual life the state of being a pupil ends, not with the expiration of years, but the moment the minor proves his fitness for being made free from the law by accepting the liberty there is in Christ Jesus. The transition, as with the Old Testament and with Christ and with the disciples, comes when the time is fulfilled and all things are now ready.

What is one to do to be made ready? Accept your death to sin in Christ and act it out. Acknowledge the sentence of death on everything that is of nature. Take and keep the place before God of utter unworthiness and helplessness. Fall down before Him in humility, meekness, patience, and resignation to His will and mercy. Fix your heart on the great and mighty God. In His grace He will work in you above what you can ask or think and will make you a monument of His mercy.

Believe that every blessing of the Covenant of grace is yours. By the death of the Testator you are entitled to it all. Act on that faith, knowing that all is yours. The new heart is yours, the law written in the heart is yours, and the Holy Spirit, the seal of the Covenant, is yours. Act on the faith and count on God as faithful, able, and so loving to reveal and make true in you all the power and glory of His everlasting Covenant.

Chapter 9

THE BLOOD OF THE COVENANT

"Behold the blood of the covenant which the Lord hath made with you" —Exodus 24:8.

"This cup is the new testament in my blood"—1 Corinthians 11:25.

"The blood of the covenant, wherewith he was sanctified" —Hebrews 10:29.

"The blood of the everlasting covenant"—Hebrews 13:20.

The blood is one of the strangest, deepest, mightiest, and most heavenly of the thoughts of God. It lies at the very root of both Covenants, but especially of the New Covenant. The difference between the two Covenants is the difference between the blood of beasts and the blood of the Lamb of God! The power of the New Covenant has no lesser measure than the worth of the blood of the Son of God!

Your Christian experience should know no standard of peace with God, purity from sin, and power over the world than the blood of Christ can give! If we want to truly and fully enter into all the

New Covenant is meant to be to us, let us ask God to reveal the worth and power of the blood of the Covenant—the precious blood of Christ!

A Blood Sacrifice

The First Covenant was also brought in with blood. There could be no covenant of friendship between a holy God and sinful men without atonement and reconciliation. There could be no atonement without death as the penalty of sin. God said: "I have given it to you upon the altar to make an atonement for your souls: for it is the blood that maketh an atonement for the soul" (Leviticus 17:11). The blood shed in death meant the death of a sacrifice slain for the sin of man. The blood sprinkled on the altar meant that God accepted this vicarious death as atonement for the sin. There is no forgiveness, no covenant, without bloodshedding.

All this was but a type and shadow of what was one day to become a mysterious reality. No thought of man or angel could have conceived what now passes all understanding—the eternal Son of God took flesh and blood and shed that blood as the blood of the New Covenant. He did this not merely to ratify it but to open the way for it and to make it possible. Even more, He did it to be, in time and eternity, the living power by which entrance into the Covenant was to be obtained and all life in it be secured.

Until we learn to form an expectation of life in the New Covenant, according to the inconceivable worth and power of the blood of God's Son, we can never have an insight into the entirely supernatural and heavenly life that a child of God may live. Let us think for a moment about the threefold light in which Scripture teaches us to regard it.

The Blood Of The New Covenant

In Hebrews 9:15 we read: "And for this cause He (Christ) is the Mediator of the new testament, that by means of death, for the redemption of the transgressions that were under the first testament, they which are called might receive the promise of the eternal inheritance." The sins of the ages of the First Covenant, which had only figuratively been atoned for, had accumulated before God. A death was needed for the redemption of these sins. In that death and bloodshedding by the Lamb of God not only were these atoned for, but the power of all sin was broken forever.

The blood of the New Covenant is redemption blood, a purchase price and ransom from the power of sin and the law. In any purchase made on earth the transference of property from the old owner to the new is complete. Its worth may be so great and the hold on it so strong, that if the price is paid, it is gone forever from him who owned it. The hold sin had on us was terrible. No one can realize its legitimate claim on us under God's law or its awful tyrant power in enslaving us.

But, the blood of God's Son has been paid. "Ye were not redeemed with corruptible things, as silver and gold, from your vain conversation received by tradition from your fathers; but with the precious blood of Christ, as of a lamb without blemish and without spot" (1 Peter 1:18-19). We have been rescued, ransomed, and redeemed entirely and eternally out of our old natural life of being under the power of sin.

Sin does not have the slightest claim on us or the slightest power over us except as our ignorance, unbelief, or half-heartedness allows it to have dominion. Our New Covenant birthright is to stand in the freedom with which Christ has made us free. Until the soul sees, accepts, desires, and claims the redemption and liberty which the blood of the Son of God has for its purchase price, measure, and security, it can never fully live the New Covenant life.

The bloodshedding for our redemption is as wonderful as the blood-sprinkling for our cleansing. Here is another one of the spiritual mysteries of the New Covenant, which loses its power when understood in human wisdom instead of the ministering of the Spirit of life. When Scripture speaks of "having our hearts sprinkled from an evil conscience," of "the blood of Christ cleansing our conscience," of our singing here on earth, "to Him that washed us from our sins in His blood" (Revelation 1:5), it brings this mighty, quickening blood of the Lamb into direct contact with our hearts.

It gives the assurance that the infinite worth of that blood in its divine sin-cleansing power can keep us clean in our walk in the sight and light of

God. As this blood of the New Covenant is known, trusted, waited for, and received from God in its divine, mighty operation in the heart, we will begin to believe that the blessed promise of a New Covenant life and walk can be fulfilled.

There is one more thing Scripture teaches concerning this blood of the New Covenant. When the Jews contrasted Moses with our Lord Jesus He said, "Except ye eat the flesh of the Son of man, and drink His blood, ye have no life in you. . . .He that eateth My flesh, and drinketh My blood, dwelleth in Me, and I in him" (John 6:53,56). As if the redeeming, sprinkling, washing, and sanctifying does not sufficiently express the intense inwardness of its action and power to permeate our whole being, the drinking of this precious blood is declared to be indispensable to having life. If we move deep into the Spirit and power of the New Covenant, let us by the Holy Spirit drink deep of this cup—the cup of the New Covenant in His blood.

Cleansing Blood

Because of sin there could be no covenant between man and God without blood and no New Covenant without the blood of the Son of God. The cleansing of sins was the first condition in making a covenant and the first condition of entrance into it. It has been found that a deeper appropriation of the blessings of the Covenant must be preceded by a new and deeper cleansing from sin. In Ezekiel 36:25 we know that the words about God's causing us to walk in His statutes are preceded by *"From all your filthiness, and from your idols, will I cleanse you."*

And then later we read in Ezekiel 37:23,26, "Neither shall they defile themselves any more with. . .any of their transgressions. . .*I will cleanse them:* so shall they be My people, and I will be their God. . .Moreover, I will make a Covenant of peace with them; it shall be an everlasting Covenant with them." The confession and casting away and the cleansing away of sin in the blood are the indispensable, all-sufficient preparation for a life in everlasting Covenant with God.

Many people feel they do not understand or realize this wonderful power of the blood. Thought and prayer do not appear to bring the light they seek. The blood of Christ is a divine mystery that passes all thought. Like every spiritual and heavenly blessing, this also needs to be imparted to us by the Holy Spirit. It was through the eternal Spirit that Christ offered the sacrifice in which the blood was shed.

Prepared For The Spirit

The blood had the life of Christ and the life of the Spirit in it. The outpouring of the blood for us was to prepare the way for the outpouring of the Spirit on us. It is the Holy Spirit alone who can minister the blood of the everlasting Covenant in power. Just as He leads the soul to the initial faith in the pardon that blood has purchased and the peace it gives, He further leads to the knowledge and experience of its cleansing power. Here again, by a faith in a heavenly power, which the soul does not fully understand and cannot define, the action which it knows is an operation of God's mighty power and effects a cleansing that gives a clean heart. This clean heart is known and accepted by the same faith, apart from signs or feelings, from sense or reason. It is experienced in joy and fellowship with God. Let us believe in the blood of the everlasting Covenant and the cleansing the Holy Spirit ministers. Let us believe in the ministry of the Holy Spirit until our whole life in the New Covenant becomes entirely His work to the glory of the Father and of Christ.

The blood of the Covenant, mystery of mysteries! Grace above all grace! O mighty power of God, open the way into the holiest, our hearts, and the New Covenant where the Holy One and our heart meets! Let us ask God, by His Holy Spirit, to teach us what the blood of the Covenant means and works.

Chapter 10

JESUS, THE MEDIATOR OF THE NEW COVENANT

"I give thee for a covenant of the people"—
Isaiah 42:6.

"The Lord, whom ye seek, shall suddenly come to his temple, even the Messenger of the covenant, whom ye delight in"—Malachi 3:1.

"Jesus was made a Surety of a better testament" —Hebrews 7:22.

"The Mediator of a better covenant, which was established upon better promises. . . The Mediator of the new testament. . .Ye are come to Jesus the Mediator of the new covenant"—Hebrews 8:6; 9:15; 12:24.

Here we have four titles given to our Lord Jesus in connection with the New Covenant. He is Himself called a Covenant. The union between God and man, which the Covenant aims at, was worked out in Him personally. In Him the reconciliation between the human and divine was perfectly effected. In Him His people find the Covenant with all its blessings. He is all that God has to give and is the assurance that it is given.

He is called the Messenger of the Covenant because He came to establish and proclaim it.

He is the Surety of the Covenant not only because He paid our debt, but also because He is Surety to us for God, that God will fulfill His part. And He is Surety for us with God that we will fulfill our part.

Finally, He is Mediator of the Covenant. As the Covenant was established in His atoning blood, is administered and applied by Him, is entered in alone by faith in Him, so it is known only through the power of His resurrection life and His never-ceasing intercession. All these names point to the one truth that in the New Covenant Christ is all in all.

Entering Into The Blessings

The subject is so large that it would be impossible to enter into all the various aspects of this precious truth. Christ's work in atonement and intercession, His bestowal of pardon and the Holy Spirit, and His daily communication of grace and strength are truths which lie at the very foundation of the faith of Christians. We do not need to speak about them here. What especially needs to be made clear is how, by faith in Christ as the Mediator of the New Covenant, we actually have access to and enter into the enjoyment of all its promised blessings.

We have already seen in studying the New Covenant how all these blessings culminate in one thing. The heart of man is to be put right. This is the only possible way for him to live in the favor of God and for God's love to find its satisfaction in him. He is to fear God, love God with all his strength, obey God, and keep all His statutes.

All that Christ did and does has this for its aim. All the higher blessings of peace and fellowship flow from this. In this, God's saving power and love find the highest proof of their triumph over sin. Nothing reveals the grace of God, the power of Jesus Christ, the reality of salvation, and the blessedness of the New Covenant as the heart of a believer where sin once abounded and where grace now abounds more exceedingly within it.

I do not know how I can better illustrate the glory of our blessed Lord Jesus as He accomplishes the real object of His redeeming work and takes entire possession of the heart He has brought, won, and washed as a dwelling for His Father than by pointing out the place He takes and the work He does in a soul. This soul is being led out of the Old Covenant bondage with its failure into the real experience of the promise and power of the New Covenant and its blessings. (See Note D.)

Attaining The Blessings

In studying the work of the Mediator in an individual, we can form a truer conception of the real glory and greatness of the work He actually accomplishes than when we merely think of the work He has done for all. It is in the application of the redemption in the life here on earth where sin abounded that its power is seen. Let us see how the entrance into the New Covenant blessing is attained.

The first step toward it in one who has been truly converted and assured of his acceptance with God is the sense of sin. He sees that the New Covenant promises are not made true in his experience. Not only is there indwelling sin but also temper, self-will, worldliness, and other known transgressions of God's law. The obedience to which God calls and will fit him, the life of abiding in Christ's love which is his privilege, the power for a holy walk, well-pleasing to God—in all this his conscience condemns him. It is in this conviction of sin that any thought or desire of the full New Covenant blessing must have its beginning.

The thought that obedience is impossible and nothing but a life of failure and self-condemnation is possible has brought about a secret despair of deliverance or a contentment with our present state. In this state it is vain to speak of God's promise or power. The heart does not respond. It knows well enough that the liberty spoken about is a dream. Where the dissatisfaction with our state has worked a longing for something better, the heart is open to receive the message.

The New Covenant is meant to be the deliverance from the power of sin. A keen longing for this is the indispensable preparation for entering fully into the Covenant.

Now comes the second step. The mind is

directed to the literal meaning of the terms of the New Covenant in its promises of cleansing from sin, a heart filled with God's fear and law, and a power to keep God's commands and never depart from Him. The eye is fixed on Jesus the Surety of the Covenant, who will Himself make it all true. As witnesses declare how, after years of bondage, all this has been fulfilled in them, the longing begins to grow into a hope. They inquire about what is needed to enter this blessed life.

Another step follows. The heart-searching question is asked: are we willing to give up every evil habit, all our own self-will, all that is of the world, and surrender ourselves to be wholly and exclusively for Jesus? God cannot take complete possession of a man, bless him so wonderfully, and work in him so mightily unless He has him completely and wholly for Himself. Happy is the man who is ready for any sacrifice.

The last step is the simplest and yet often the most difficult. Here we need to know Jesus as Mediator of the Covenant. As we hear of the life of holiness, obedience, and victory over sin, which the Covenant promises, and realize that it will be to us according to our faith, our heart often fails because of fear. I am willing, but do I have the power to make and maintain this full surrender? Do I have the power and strong faith to grasp and hold this offered blessing so that it will be and continue to be mine? How such questions perplex the soul until it finds the answer to them in the one word, Jesus! *He will bestow the power to make the surrender and believe.*

This is as surely and exclusively His work as atonement and intercession are His alone. As sure as it was His to win and ascend to the throne, it is His to prove His dominion in the individual soul. He, the Living One, is in divine power to work and maintain the life of communion and victory within us. He is the Mediator and Surety of the Covenant. He is the God-man who has undertaken not only for all that God requires but for all that we need as well.

Claiming The Promises

When this is seen, the believer learns that here, just as at conversion, it is all by faith. With the eyes fixed on some promise of the New Covenant, we need now to turn from self and anything it could or needs to do, let go of self, and fall into the arms of Jesus. He is the Mediator of the New Covenant. He leads us into it.

With the assurance that Jesus and every New Covenant blessing is already ours because we are God's children, we must claim God's promises. With the desire to appropriate and enjoy what we have allowed to lie unused, we must ask God's guidance. With the faith that Jesus gives us the needed strength to claim and accept our heritage as a present possession, the will boldly dares to do the deed and take the heavenly gift. This gift is a life in Christ according to the better promises. By faith in Jesus you have seen and received Him as the Mediator of the New Covenant both in heaven and in your heart. He is the Mediator who makes it true between God *and you* as your experience.

Sometimes the fear has been expressed that, if we urgently seek the work the Spirit does in the heart, we may be drawn away from trusting in what He has done and is doing by what we are experiencing of its working. The answer is simple. It is *with the heart alone* that Christ truly can be known or honored. The work of grace and the saving power of Christ is to be done and displayed in the heart. It is *in the heart* alone that the Holy Spirit has His sphere of work. There He is to work Christ's likeness. It is *there* alone He can glorify Christ.

The Spirit can only glorify Christ by revealing His saving power *in us*. If we were to speak of what *we are to do* in cleansing our heart and keeping it right, the fear would be well-grounded. But, the New Covenant calls us to the very opposite. What it tells us of the atonement and righteousness of God it has won for us will be our only glory even amid the highest holiness of heaven. Christ's work of holiness here in the heart can only deepen the consciousness of that righteousness as our only plea. The sanctification of the Spirit, as the fulfillment of the New Covenant promises, is a taking of the things of Christ and revealing and imparting them to us.

The deeper our entrance into and possession of the New Covenant gift of a new heart, the fuller our knowledge and love of Him who is its Mediator will be, the more we will glory in Him alone.

The Covenant deals with the heart so that Christ may be found there and *dwell there by faith.* As we look at the heart, not in the light of feeling or experience but in the light of the faith of God's Covenant, we will learn to think and speak of it as God does. We will begin to know what it is. There Christ manifests Himself and He and the Father come to make their abode.

Chapter 11

JESUS, THE SURETY OF THE BETTER COVENANT

"And inasmuch as not without an oath he was made priest. . .By so much was Jesus made a Surety of a better covenant. . .Wherefore he is able also to save them to the uttermost that come unto God by him, seeing he ever liveth to make intercession for them" —Hebrews 7:20,22,25.

A *surety* is one who stands good for another so that a certain engagement will be faithfully performed. Jesus is the Surety of the New Covenant. He stands surety with us for God so that God's part in the Covenant will faithfully be performed. And, He stands surety with God for us so that our part will also be faithfully performed.

Jesus As Surety

If we are to live in covenant with God, everything depends upon our knowing correctly what Jesus secures to us. The more we know and trust Him, the more assured our faith will be that its every promise and demand will be fulfilled. We will be assured that a life of faithful keeping of God's Covenant is indeed possible because Jesus is the Surety of the Covenant. He makes God's faithfulness and ours equally sure.

We read that it was because His priesthood was confirmed by the oath of God that He became the Surety of a much better Covenant. The oath of God gives us the security that His suretyship will secure all the better promises. The meaning and infinite value of God's oath has been explained in the previous chapter. "An oath for confirmation is to them an end of all strife. Wherein God, willing more abundantly to shew unto the heirs of promise the immutability of His counsel, confirmed it by an oath: that by two immutable things, in which it was impossible for God to lie, we might have a strong consolation" (Hebrews 6:16-18).

We have a Covenant with certain definite promises, and we have Jesus as the Surety of that Covenant. We also have perfect confidence in the unchangeableness of the counsel and promise of the living God coming in between with an oath. Can we not see that the one thing God aims at in this Covenant and asks with regard to it is an absolute confidence that He is going to do all He has promised however difficult or wonderful it may appear?

His oath is an end to all fear or doubt. Let no one think of understanding the Covenant, judging or saying what may be expected from it, much less experiencing its blessings, until he meets God with an Abraham-like faith. Be fully assured that what He has promised He is able to perform. The Covenant is a sealed mystery, except to the soul who is going without reserve to trust God and abandon itself to His Word and work.

Our passage tells us about the work of Christ, the Surety of the better Covenant. Because of this priesthood confirmed by oath, He is able to completely save those who draw near to God through Him. He can do this because "He ever liveth to make intercession for them" (Hebrews 7:25). As Surety of the Covenant, He is ceaselessly engaged in watching their needs, presenting them to the Father, receiving His answer, and imparting its blessing.

It is because of this never-ceasing mediation, receiving and transmitting from God to us the gifts and powers of the heavenly world, that He is able to save completely. Because of this He is able to work and maintain in us a salvation as complete as God is willing it should be and as complete as the better Covenant has assured us it will be in the better promises upon which it was established. These promises are expounded (Hebrews 8:7-13) as being none other than those of the New Covenant of Jeremiah, with the law written in the heart by the Spirit of God as our experience of the power of that salvation.

Christ—Our Assurance

Jesus, the Surety of a better Covenant, is to be our assurance that everything connected with the

Covenant is unchangeably and eternally sure. Jesus is the keynote of all our fellowship with God, all our prayers and desires, and all our life and walk. With full assurance of faith and hope we can look for every word of the Covenant to be made fully true to us by God's own power. Let us look at some of these things we are to be fully assured of if we are to breathe the spirit of children of the New Covenant.

There is the love of God. The very thought of a Covenant is an alliance of friendship. It is a means of assuring us of His love, drawing us close to His heart of love, getting our hearts under the power of His love and filled with it. It is because God loves us with an infinite love, wants us to know it and give it complete liberty to bestow itself on us, and bless us that the New Covenant has been made and God's own Son been made its Surety.

This love of God is an infinite divine energy doing its utmost to fill the soul with itself and its blessedness. God's Son is the Messenger of this love. He is the Surety of the Covenant in which God reveals it to us. Let us learn that the chief need in studying the Covenant, keeping it, and seeking and claiming its blessings is the exercise of a strong, confident assurance in God's love.

Then there is the assurance of the sufficiency of Christ's finished redemption. All that was needed to put away sin and free us entirely and forever from its power has been accomplished by Christ. His blood, death, resurrection, and ascension have taken us out of the power of the world and transplanted us into a new life in the power of the heavenly world. All this is divine reality. Christ is Surety that the divine righteousness, acceptance, and all-sufficient grace and strength are always ours. He is Surety that all these can and will be communicated to us in unbroken continuance.

It is also true with the assurance of what is needed on our part to enter into this life in the New Covenant. We shrink back either from the surrender of all because we do not know whether we have the power to let it go or from the faith because we fear ours will never be as strong or bold to take and hold all that is offered to us in this wonderful Covenant. Jesus is Surety of a better Covenant. The better consists in this very thing, that it undertakes to provide the children of the Covenant with the very dispositions they need to accept and enjoy it.

A Heart Surrendered To God

We have seen how the heart is the central object of the Covenant promise. Jesus is the Surety of a heart circumcised to love God completely and into which God's law and fear have been put *so that it will not depart from Him*. Let us repeat: The one thing God asks of us and has given the Covenant and its Surety to secure—*the confident trust that all will be done in us that is needed*—is what we dare not withhold.

I think some of us are beginning to see what our great mistake has been. We have thought and spoken great things of what Christ did on the cross and does on the throne as Covenant Surety. But, we have stopped there. *We have not expected Him to do great things in our hearts*. Yet it is there, in our heart, that the consummation of the work on the cross and the throne takes place. In the heart the New Covenant has its full triumph. The Surety is to be known not by what the mind can think of Him in heaven, but by what He does to make Himself known in the heart. *There* is the place where His love triumphs and is enthroned.

Let us believe and receive Him with the heart as the Covenant Surety. With every desire we entertain in connection with it, every duty it calls us to, and every promise it holds out, let us look to Jesus, under God's oath the Surety of the Covenant. Let us believe that by the Holy Spirit the heart is His home and throne. If we have not done it yet, in a definite act of faith, let us throw ourselves utterly on Him for our entire New Covenant life and walk. No surety was ever so faithful to his undertaking *as Jesus will be to His on our behalf, in our hearts*.

Offer Yourself In Weakness

In spite of the strong confidence and consolation the oath of God and the Surety of the Covenant gives, there are some still looking wistfully at this blessed life. They are still afraid to trust themselves to this wondrous grace. They have a conception of faith as something great and mighty, and they know and feel that theirs is not such. So their feebleness remains an insurmountable barrier to their inheriting the promise. Let me say again: Brother and sister, the act of faith by which you accept and enter this life in the New Covenant is not commonly an act of power. It is often of weakness, fear, and much trembling.

Even in the midst of this feebleness it is not an act in your strength. Rather, it is a secret and perhaps unfelt strength which Jesus the Surety of the Covenant gives you. God has made Him Surety with the purpose of inspiring us with courage and confidence. He longs and delights to bring you into the Covenant. Why not bow before Him and say meekly: He does hear prayer. He brings souls into the Covenant. He enables a soul to believe. I can trust Him confidently.

Just begin to quietly believe that there is an Almighty Lord, given by the Father, to do everything needed to make *all* Covenant grace wholly true in you. Bow low and look up out of your low estate to your glorified Lord. Maintain your confidence that a soul who, in its nothingness, trusts in Him will receive more than it can ask or think.

Believer, come and truly be a believer. Believe that God is showing you how completely the Lord Jesus wants to have you and your life for Himself and how He is willing to take total charge of you and work all in you. Believe how entirely you can even now commit your trust, surrender, and faithfulness to the covenant, with all you are and are to be, to Him who is your Blessed Surety. If you believe, you will see the glory of God.

In a sense, measure, and power that passes

knowledge, Jesus Christ is Himself all that God can either ask or give. He is all that God wants to see in us. *"He that believeth on Me. . .out of his belly shall flow rivers of living water"* (John 7:38).

Chapter 12

THE BOOK OF THE COVENANT

"And he (Moses) took the book of the covenant, and read in the audience of the people: and they said, All that the Lord hath said will we do, and be obedient. And Moses took the blood, and sprinkled it on the people, and said, Behold the blood of the covenant which the Lord hath made with you concerning all these words"—Exodus 24:7-8.

Here is a new aspect of God's blessed Book. Before Moses sprinkled the blood, he read the Book of the Covenant and obtained the people's acceptance of it. When he had sprinkled it he said, "Behold the blood of the covenant, which the Lord hath made with you *concerning all these words*" (Exodus 24:8). The Book contained all the conditions of the Covenant. Only through the Book could they know all that God asked of them and all that they might ask of Him. Let us consider what new light can be thrown upon the Covenant and the Book by the one thought that the Bible is the Book of the Covenant. The first thought suggested will be this. The spirit of our life and experience as it lives either in the Old or New Covenant will be in nothing more manifest than in our dealings with the Book. The Old as well as the New had a book. Our Bible contains both. The New was enfolded in the Old. The Old is unfolded in the New. It is possible to read the Old in the spirit of the New. It is possible to read the New as well as the Old in the spirit of the Old.

The Spirit Of The Old Covenant

We can clearly see this spirit of the Old in Israel when the Covenant was made. At once they were ready to promise, "All that the Lord hath said will we do, and be obedient." There was so little sense of their own sinfulness or the holiness and glory of God that, with perfect self-confidence, they considered themselves able to undertake and keep the Covenant. They understood little of the meaning of the blood with which they were sprinkled or of the death and redemption of which it was the symbol. In their own strength and power of the flesh, they were ready to undertake to serve God.

It is just this spirit in which many Christians regard the Bible. It is a system of laws, a course of instruction to direct us in the way God would have us go. All He asks of us is that we do our utmost in seeking to fulfill them. We cannot do more. This we are sincerely ready to do. They know little or nothing of what death through which the Covenant is established means. They know little of what life from the dead is through which a man

92

can walk in covenant with the God of heaven.

This self-confident spirit in Israel is explained by what had previously happened. When God came down on Mount Sinai in thunderings and lightnings to give the law, they were greatly afraid. They said to Moses, "Speak thou with us, and we will hear: but let not God speak with us, lest we die" (Exodus 20:19). They thought it was simply a matter of hearing and knowing. They thought they could certainly obey. They did not know that it is only the presence, nearness, and the power of God humbling us and making us afraid that can conquer the power of sin. Only this can give the power to obey.

It is so much easier to receive the instruction from man and live than to wait and hear the voice of God and die to all our own strength and goodness. Is it any wonder that many Christians seek to live in daily contact with Him and without the faith that it is only His presence that can keep from sin? Their faith is a matter of outward instruction from man. Waiting to hear God's voice that they may obey Him and death to the flesh and the world that comes with a close walk with God are unknown. They may be faithful and diligent in the study of their Bible, in reading or hearing Bible teaching. They do not seek to have as much fellowship with the Covenant God as possible. It is fellowship which makes the Christian life possible.

The Book Of The New Covenant

If you want to be delivered from all this, learn to read the Book of the New Covenant in the New Covenant Spirit. One of the very first articles of the New Covenant refers to this matter. When God says, "I will put My law in their inward parts and write it in their hearts," He promises that the words of His Holy Book will no longer be mere outward teaching. What they command will be our very disposition and delight worked in us as a birth and life by the Holy Spirit. Every word of the New Covenant then becomes a divine assurance of what can be obtained by the Holy Spirit's working. The soul learns to see that the letter kills and the flesh profits nothing.

The study, knowledge of, and delight in Bible words and thoughts cannot profit except as the Holy Spirit is waited on to make them life. The acceptance of Holy Scripture in the letter and in the human understanding and reception of it is as fruitless as Israel's was at Sinai. But, as the Word of God, spoken by the Living God through the Spirit into the heart that waits on Him, it is found to be quick and powerful. It is a word that works effectually in those who believe, placing within the heart the actual possession of the very grace of which the Word has spoken.

The New Covenant is a ministry of the Spirit. All its teaching is meant to be teaching by the Holy Spirit. The two most remarkable chapters in the Bible on the preaching of the gospel are those in which Paul expounds the secret of his teaching (1 Corinthians 2; 2 Corinthians 3). Every minister ought to see whether he can pass his examination in them. They tell us that in the New Covenant the Holy Spirit is everything. It was the Holy Spirit entering the heart, writing, revealing, and impressing upon it God's law and truth that could work true obedience. No excellency of speech or human wisdom can profit. God must reveal to the preacher and hearer by His Holy Spirit the things He has prepared for us.

The Work Of The Spirit

What is true of the preacher is equally true of the hearer. One of the great reasons that so many Christians never come out of the Old Covenant— never even know they are in it and have to come out of it—is that there is so much head knowledge. They lack the power of the Spirit in the heart. It is only when preachers, hearers, and readers believe that the Book of the New Covenant needs the Spirit of the New Covenant to explain and apply it that the Word of God can do its work.

Learn the double lesson. What God has joined together, let no man put asunder. The Bible is the Book of the New Covenant. And, the Holy Spirit is the only minister of what belongs to the Covenant. Do not expect to understand or profit by your Bible knowledge without continually seeking the teaching of the Holy Spirit. Beware that your earnest Bible study, excellent books, or beloved teachers do not *take the place of the Holy Spirit!*

Pray daily, perseveringly, and believingly for His teaching. He will write the Word in your heart.

The Bible is the Book of the New Covenant. Ask the Holy Spirit especially to reveal the New Covenant in it to you. It is inconceivable what loss today's Church is suffering because so few believers truly live as its heirs and in the true knowledge and enjoyment of its promises.

Ask God, in humble faith, to give you in all your Bible reading the spirit of wisdom and revelation and enlightened eyes of your heart, to know what promises the Covenant reveals. Ask God to reveal the divine security in Jesus, the Surety of the Covenant, that every promise will be fulfilled in you in divine power. Ask Him to reveal the intimate fellowship to which it admits you with the God of the Covenant. Humbly waiting for and listening to the ministry of the Spirit will make the Book of the Covenant shine with new light—even the light of God's countenance and a full salvation.

Unbroken Fellowship

All this especially applies to the knowledge of what the New Covenant is actually meant to work. Amid all we hear, read, and understand of the different promises of the New Covenant, it is quite possible that we have never had that heavenly vision of it as a whole. With its overmastering power it compels acceptance. Hear once again what it really is. *The obedience and fellowship with God is now brought within our reach and offered us.*

Our Father tells us in the Book of the New Covenant that He now expects us to live in full, unbroken obedience and communion with Him. He tells us that by the mighty power of His Son and Spirit *He Himself will work this in us.* Everything has been arranged for it. He tells us that a life of unbroken obedience is possible because Christ, the Mediator, will live in us and enable us each moment to live in Him. He tells us that all He wants is the surrender of faith and the yielding of ourselves to Him to do His work.

Let us look and see *this holy life, with all its powers and blessings, coming down from God in heaven, in the Son and His Spirit.* Let us believe that the Holy Spirit can give us a vision of it, as a prepared gift to be bestowed in living power and take possession of us. Let us look upward and inward in the faith of the Son and the Spirit. God will show us that every word written in the Book of the Covenant is not only true but that it can be made spirit and truth within us and in our daily life. *This certainly can be.*

Chapter 13

NEW COVENANT OBEDIENCE

"Now therefore, if ye will obey my voice indeed, and keep my covenant, then ye shall be. . .an holy nation unto me"—Exodus 19:5.

"And the Lord thy God will circumcise thine heart, and the heart of thy seed, to love the Lord thy God with all thy heart, and with all thy soul. . . .And thou shalt return and obey the voice of the Lord, and do all his commandments"—Deuteronomy 30:6,8.

"And I will put my Spirit within you, and cause you to walk in my statutes, and ye shall keep my judgments"—Ezekiel 36:27.

In making the New Covenant God very definitely said, "Not according to the covenant that I made with their fathers" (Hebrews 8:9). We have learned the fault with that Covenant. It made God's favor dependent upon the obedience of the people. *"Obey* My voice, and I will be your God" (Jeremiah 7:23). We have learned how the New Covenant remedied the defect. God Himself provided for the obedience. It changes *"If ye keep My* judgments" into "I will put My Spirit within you, and *ye shall keep.*" Instead of the Covenant and its fulfillment depending on man's obedience, God undertakes to ensure the obedience. The Old Covenant proved the need and pointed out the path of holiness. The New inspires the love and gives the power of holiness.

In connection with this change, a serious and dangerous mistake is often made. Because the New Covenant obedience no longer occupies the place it had in the Old and free grace has replaced it, justifying the ungodly and bestowing gifts on the rebellious, many are under the impression that obedience is *no longer as indispensable as it was then.* The error is a terrible one.

Obedience Is Still Essential

The whole Old Covenant was meant to teach the lesson of the absolute, indispensable necessity of obedience for a life in God's favor. The New Covenant comes, not to provide a substitute for that obedience in faith, but through faith to secure the obedience by giving a heart that delights in it and has the power for it. Men abuse the free grace when they rest content with grace without the obedience it is meant for.

They boast of the higher privileges of the New Covenant, while its chief blessing, *the power of a holy life and a heart delighting in God's law,* and a life in which God causes and enables us by His indwelling Spirit to keep His commandments is neglected. If there is one thing we need to know well it is the place obedience takes in the New Covenant.

Let our first thought be, *Obedience is essential*. The thought of obedience lies at the very root of the relationship of a creature to his God and God admitting the creature to His fellowship. It is the only thing God spoke of in Paradise when "the Lord God commanded the man" not to eat of the forbidden fruit (Genesis 2:16). In Christ's great salvation it is the power that redeemed us. "By the obedience of one shall many be made righteous" (Romans 5:19).

In the promise of the New Covenant it takes the first place. God arranges to circumcise the hearts of His people—in the putting off of the body of the flesh in the circumcision of Christ—to love God with all their heart and obey His commandments. The crowning gift of Christ's exaltation was the Holy Spirit to bring salvation to us as an inward thing. The first Covenant demanded obedience and failed because it could not find it. *The New Covenant was expressly made to provide for obedience*. Obedience is essential to a life in the full enjoyment of the New Covenant blessing.

Obedience Overcomes Unbelief

It is this indispensable necessity of obedience that explains why so often the entrance into the full enjoyment of the New Covenant has depended upon a single act of surrender. There was some evil or doubtful habit in the life, or the conscience often said that it was not in perfect accord with

God's perfect will. Attempts were made to push aside the troublesome suggestion. Unbelief said it would be impossible to overcome the habit and maintain the promise of obedience to the Voice within.

In the meantime, all our prayer seemed to be of no avail. It was as if faith could not lay hold of the blessing which was in full sight until the soul finally consented to regard this little thing as the test of its surrender to obey in everything. It was a test of its faith that in everything the Surety of the Covenant would give power to maintain the obedience. With the evil or doubtful thing given up, a good conscience restored, and the heart's confidence before God assured, the soul could receive and possess what it sought. Obedience is essential.

Obedience is possible. The thought of a demand which man cannot possibly give up cuts at the very root of true hope and strength. The secret thought "No man can obey God" throws thousands back into the Old Covenant life and into a false peace that God does not expect more than that we do our best. Obedience is possible. The entire New Covenant promises and secures this.

Only understand what obedience means. The renewed man still has the flesh with its evil nature out of which involuntary evil thoughts and dispositions arise. These may be found in a truly obedient man. Obedience deals with doing what is known to be God's will as taught by the Word, the Holy Spirit, and conscience. When George Mueller spoke of the great happiness he had for more than sixty years in God's service, he attributed it to two things. First, he had loved God's Word, and then "he had maintained a good conscience, not willfully going on in a course he knew to be contrary to the mind of God."

When the full revelation of God broke on Gerhard Tersteggen he wrote, "I promise, with Thy help and power, rather to give up the last drop of my blood, than knowingly and willingly in my heart or my life be untrue and disobedient to Thee." Such obedience is an attainable degree of grace.

Obedience is possible. When the law is written in the heart, the heart is circumcised to love the Lord with all our heart and obey Him. When the love of God is shed abroad in the heart, it means that the love of God's law and Himself has now become the moving power of our life. This love is no vague sentiment in man's imagination of something that exists in heaven. It is a living, mighty power of God in the heart, working effectually according to His working, which works mightily in us. A life of obedience is possible.

This obedience is of faith. "By faith Abraham. . . obeyed" (Hebrews 11:8). By faith the promises of the Covenant, the presence of the Surety of the Covenant, the hidden inworking of the Holy Spirit, and the love of God in His infinite desire and power to make true in us all His love and promises must live in us. Faith can bring them near and make us live in the very midst of them.

Christ and His wonderful redemption do not need to remain at a distance from us in heaven but can become our continual experience.

However cold or feeble we may feel, faith knows that the new heart is in us. The love of God's law is our very nature, and the teaching and power of the Spirit are within us. Such faith knows it can obey. Let us hear the voice of our Savior, the Surety of the Covenant, as He says with a deeper, fuller meaning than when He was on earth: "Only believe. If thou canst believe, all things are possible to him that believeth."

Last of all, let us understand, *Obedience is a joy and a delight.* Do not regard it only as *the way* to the joy and blessing of the New Covenant. Regard it, in its very nature, as part of that blessedness. To have the voice of God teaching and guiding you, be united to God in willing what He wills, working out what He works in you by His Spirit, doing His holy will, and pleasing Him. All this is joy unspeakable and full of glory.

New Covenant Obedience

To a healthy man it is a delight to walk or work, to put forth his strength and conquer difficulties. To a sick man it is bondage and weariness. The Old Covenant demanded obedience with an unrelenting *must* and the threat that followed it. The New Covenant changes the must to *can* and *may*.

Ask God by the Holy Spirit to show you how "you have been created in Christ Jesus unto good works" (Ephesians 2:10). Ask how, as fitted as a vine is for bearing grapes, your new nature is perfectly prepared for every good work. Ask Him to show you that He means obedience to be possible and also the most delightful, attractive gift He has to bestow. It is the entrance into His love and all its blessedness.

In the New Covenant the most important thing is not the wonderful treasure of strength and grace it contains nor the divine security that the treasure never can fail. But, it is that the living God gives Himself, makes Himself known, and takes possession of us as our God. Man was created for this. For this He was redeemed again. So that it may be our actual experience, the Holy Spirit has been given and is dwelling in us. Obedience is the blessed link between what God has already worked in us and what He waits to work. Let us seek to walk before Him in the consciousness that we are one of those who live in noble, holy consciousness. My one work is to obey God.

Why do so many believers see so little of the beauty of this New Covenant life with its power of holy, joyful obedience? "Their eyes were holden that they should not know Him" (Luke 24:16). The Lord was with the disciples, but their hearts were blind. It is still this way. Like Elisha's servant, all heaven is around him, and he does not know it. Nothing will help but the prayer, "Lord, I pray Thee, open his eyes, that he may see" (2 Kings 6:17). Lord, is there someone reading this who just needs one touch to see it all? Give that touch!

Listen, brethren. Your Father loves you with an infinite love and longs to make you His holy, happy, obedient child. Hear His message. He has an entirely different life for you than what you are living. *He gives a life in which His grace will actually work in you every moment all He asks you to be.* He brings a life of simple, childlike obedience, doing for the day just what the Father shows you to be His will. He offers a life in which the abiding love of your Father, the abiding presence of your Savior, and the joy of the Holy Spirit can keep and make you glad and strong.

This is His message. This life is for you. Do not be afraid to accept this life. Give yourself to it and its entire obedience. In Christ it is possible. It is sure.

Brothers and sisters, just look heavenward and ask the Father, by the Holy Spirit, to show you the beautiful heavenly life. Ask and expect it. Keep your eyes fixed upon it. *The great blessing of the New Covenant is obedience. It is the wonderful power to will and do as God wills.* It is the entrance to every other blessing. It is paradise restored and heaven opened—the creature honoring his Creator and the Creator delighting in His creature. It is the child glorifying the Father and the Father glorifying the child as He changes him from glory to glory into the likeness of His Son.

Chapter 14

THE NEW COVENANT: A COVENANT OF GRACE

"Sin shall not have dominion over you: for ye are not under the law, but under grace"— Romans 6:14.

Covenant of grace, though not found in Scripture, is the correct expression of the truth it abundantly teaches. The contrast between the two covenants is none other than that of law and grace. Grace is the great characteristic of the New Covenant. "The law entered that the offence might abound. But where sin abounded, grace did much more abound" (Romans 5:20). To bring the Romans entirely away from under the Old Covenant and teach them their place in the New, Paul writes, "Ye are not under the law, but under grace."

He assures them that if they believe this and live in it, their experience would confirm God's promise: "Sin shall not have dominion over you." What the law could not do—give deliverance from the power of sin over us—grace would effect. The

New Covenant was entirely a Covenant of grace. It had its origin in the wonderful grace of God. It was meant to be a manifestation of the riches and the glory of that grace. Of and by grace working in us, all its promises can be fulfilled and experienced.

The Abundance Of Grace

The word *grace* is used in two senses. First it is the gracious disposition in God *which moves Him* to love us freely without our merit and bestow all His blessings upon us. Then it also means that power which this grace bestows upon us to work in us. The redeeming work of Christ and the righteousness He won for us together with the work of the Spirit in us as the power of the new life are spoken of as *grace*. It includes all that Christ has done and still does, all He has and gives, and all He is for us and in us. John says, "We beheld His glory, the glory as of the only begotten of the Father, full of grace and truth" (John 1:14). The law was given by Moses. Grace and truth came by Jesus Christ. "And of His fullness have all we received, and grace for grace" (John 1:16). What the law demands, grace supplies.

The contrast which John pointed out is expounded by Paul. "The law came in, that the offence might abound" and the way be more exceedingly prepared for the abounding of grace. The law points the way but gives no strength to walk in it. It demands but makes no provision for its demands being met. The law burdens, condemns, and slays. It can awaken desire but not satisfy it. It can rouse to effort but not secure success. It can appeal to motives but gives no inward power beyond what man himself has. So, while warring against sin, it became its very ally in giving the sinner over to a hopeless condemnation. "The strength of sin is the law" (1 Corinthians 15:56).

To deliver us from the bondage and dominion of sin, grace came by Jesus Christ. Its work is twofold. Its exceeding abundance is seen in the free, full pardon of all transgression, the bestowal of a perfect righteousness, and the acceptance into God's favor and friendship. "In whom we have redemption through His blood, the forgiveness of sins, according to the riches of His grace" (Ephesians 1:7). It is not only at conversion when we are admitted into God's favor, but throughout our life, that we owe everything to grace, and grace alone. The thought of merit and work and worthiness is forever excluded.

The exceeding abundance of grace is equally seen in the work which the Holy Spirit maintains every moment within us. We have found that the central blessing of the New Covenant, flowing from Christ's redemption and the pardon of our sins, is the new heart in which God's law, fear, and love have been put. It is in the fulfillment of this promise, *in the maintenance of the heart in a state of meetness for God's indwelling,* that the glory of grace is especially seen. In the very nature of things this must be so.

Grace Reigns In The Heart

Paul writes, "Where sin abounded, grace did much more abound" (Romans 5:20). And where, as far as I was concerned, did sin abound? All the sin in earth and hell could not harm me if it were not present in my heart. There it has exercised its terrible dominion. There the exceeding abundance of grace must be proved if it is to benefit me. All grace in heart and heaven could not help me. It is only in the heart that it can be received, known, and enjoyed.

"Where sin abounded" in the heart, "grace did much more abound. As sin hath reigned unto death," working its destruction in the heart and life, "even so might grace reign" in the heart "through righteousness unto eternal life by Jesus Christ our Lord." As has been said before, "They that receive the abundance of grace shall reign in life through Jesus Christ."

Scripture speaks wondrous things about this reign in the heart. Paul speaks of the grace that prepared him for his work, of "that gift of the grace of God given unto me by the effectual working of His power" (Ephesians 3:7). "The grace of our Lord was exceeding abundant with faith and love" (1 Timothy 1:14). *"His grace* which was bestowed upon me was not in vain; but I *laboured more abundantly* than they all: yet not I, but *the grace* of God which was with me" (1 Corinthians 15:10). "He said unto me, *My grace* is sufficient for thee: for My strength is made perfect in weakness" (2 Corinthians 12:9).

He speaks in the same way about grace as working in the life of believers when he exhorts them to "be strong in the grace that is in Christ Jesus" (2 Timothy 2:1). He tells us of "the grace of God" exhibited in the liberality of the Macedonian Christians and "the exceeding grace of God" in the Corinthians. He encourages them, "God is able to make all grace abound toward you; that ye. . .may abound to every good work" (2 Corinthians 9:8).

Grace is not only the power that moves the heart of God in its compassion toward us, when He acquits and accepts the sinner and makes him a child. It is also the power that moves the heart of the saint and provides it each moment with just the disposition and the power which it needs to love God and do His will.

Sanctifying Grace

It is impossible to speak of the wonderful, free, sufficient grace that pardons without speaking of the grace that sanctifies. We are just as dependent upon the latter as the former. We can do as little to the one as the other. The grace that works in us must exclusively do all in and through us as the grace that pardons does all for us. In both cases everything is by faith alone. Not to comprehend this brings a double danger.

On the one hand, people think that grace cannot be more exalted than in the bestowal of pardon on the vile and unworthy. A secret feeling arises that if God is magnified by our sins more than anything else, we must not expect to be freed from them in this life. With many this cuts at the root of the life of true holiness. On the other hand, from not knowing that grace always and alone does all the work in our sanctification and fruit-bearing, men are thrown on their own efforts. Their life remains one of feebleness and bondage under the law, and they never yield themselves to let grace do all it would.

Let us listen to what God's Word says. *"By grace* are ye saved *through faith*. . .not of works, lest any man should boast. For we are His workmanship, created in Christ Jesus unto good works, which God hath before ordained that we should walk in them" (Ephesians 2:8-10). Grace stands in contrast to our own good works not only before conversion but after conversion, too. We are created *in Christ Jesus* for good works, which God had prepared for us. Grace alone can work them in us and work them out through us. The work of grace is not only the commencement but also the continuance of the Christian life.

"And if by grace, then is it no more of works: otherwise grace is no more grace. But if it be of works, then it is no more grace: otherwise work is no more work" (Romans 11:6). As we see that grace literally and absolutely does all in us, so that all our actions are the showing forth of grace in us, we will consent to live the life of faith in which every moment, everything is expected from God. It is only then that we will experience that sin will never for a moment have dominion over us.

"Ye are not under the law, but under grace" (Romans 6:14). There are three possible lives: one entirely under the law; one entirely under grace; and one a mixed life, partly law, partly grace. It is against this last which Paul warns the Romans. It is this which is so common and works such ruin among Christians. Let us find out whether this is our position and the cause of our low state. Let us ask God to open our eyes by the Holy Spirit to see that in the New Covenant everything—every movement, every moment of our Christian life—is of abounding grace working mightily. Let us believe that our Covenant God waits to cause all grace to abound toward us. Let us begin to live the life of faith that depends upon, trusts in, looks to, and ever waits for God, through Jesus Christ by the Holy Spirit, to work in us that which is pleasing in His sight.

Grace to you and peace be multiplied!

Chapter 15

THE COVENANT OF AN EVERLASTING PRIESTHOOD

"That my covenant might be with Levi, saith the Lord of hosts. My covenant was with him of life and peace; and I gave them to him for the fear wherewith he feared me, and was afraid before my name. The law of truth was in his mouth, and iniquity was not found in his lips: he walked with me in peace and equity, and did turn many away from iniquity"—Malachi 2:4-6.

God meant Israel to be a nation of priests. In the first making of the Covenant this was distinctly stipulated. "If ye will obey My voice indeed, and keep My covenant. . .ye shall be unto Me a kingdom of priests" (Exodus 19:5,6). They were to be the stewards of the oracles of God and the channels through whom God's knowledge and blessing were to be communicated to the world. In them all nations were to be blessed.

Within the people of Israel one tribe was especially set apart to embody and emphasize the priestly idea. The firstborn sons of the entire nation were to have been the priests. But, to secure a more complete separation from the rest of the people and the entire giving up of any share in their possessions and pursuits, God chose one tribe to be exclusively devoted to the work of proving what constitutes the spirit and power of priesthood. Just as the priesthood of the entire nation was part of God's Covenant with them, so the special calling of Levi is spoken of as God's Covenant of life and peace being with Him. It is the Covenant of an everlasting priesthood. All this was to be a picture to help them and us to understand the priesthood of His own blessed Son, the Mediator of the New Covenant.

The Call To Priesthood

Like Israel, under the New Covenant all God's people are a royal priesthood. The right of free and full access to God—the duty and power of mediating for our fellow-men and being God's channel of blessing to them—is the inalienable birthright of every believer. Because of the feebleness of many of God's children and their ignorance of the mighty grace of the New Covenant, they are utterly unable to exercise their priestly functions. To make up for this lack of service, through the exceeding riches of His grace and the power He gives men to become His followers, God still allows and invites those redeemed ones who are willing to offer their lives to this blessed ministry.

To the one who accepts the call, the New Covenant brings in special measure what God has said: "My Covenant was with him of life and peace" (Malachi 2:5). It becomes to him "the Covenant of an everlasting priesthood" (Numbers 25:13). As the Covenant of Levi's priesthood issued and culminated in Christ's, ours issues from that again and receives from it its blessing to dispense to the world.

Conditions Of Priesthood

To those who desire to know the conditions on which the Covenant of an everlasting priesthood can be received and carried out, a study of the conditions on which Levi received the priesthood will be most instructive. Not only are we told that God chose that tribe but what there especially was in that tribe that prepared it for the work. Malachi says, "My covenant was with him of life and peace; and I gave them to him for the fear wherewith he feared Me, and was afraid before My name" (Malachi 2:5). The reference is to what took place at Sinai when Israel had made the golden calf.

Moses called all who were on the Lord's side and who were ready to avenge the dishonor done to God to come to him. The tribe of Levi did so, and at his bidding took their swords and slew three thousand of the idolatrous people (Exodus 32:26-29). In the blessing with which Moses blessed the tribes before his death, their absolute devotion to God, without considering relative or friend, is mentioned as the proof of their readiness for God's service. In Deuteronomy 33:8-9 it says:

"Let Thy Thummin and Thy Urim be with Thy holy one. . .who said unto his father and to his mother, I have not seen him; neither did he acknowledge his brethren, nor knew his own children: for they have observed Thy word, and kept Thy covenant."

The same principle is strikingly illustrated in the story of Aaron's grandson, Phinehas, where, in his zeal for God, he executed judgment on disobedience to God's command. The words are most suggestive. "And the Lord spake unto Moses, saying, Phinehas, the son of Eleazer, the son of Aaron the priest hath turned My wrath away from the children of Israel, while he was zealous for My sake among them, that I consumed not the children of Israel in My jealousy. Wherefore say, Behold, I give unto him My covenant of peace: and he shall have it, and his seed after him, even the covenant of an everlasting priesthood; because *he was zealous for his God,* and made an atonement for the children of Israel" (Numbers 25:10-13).

The gate into the Covenant of an everlasting priesthood is to be jealous with God's jealousy— to be jealous for God's honor and rise up against sin. It is the secret of being entrusted by God with the sacred work of teaching His people, burning incense before Him, and turning many from iniquity (Deuteronomy 33:10; Malachi 2:6).

Even the New Covenant is in danger of being abused by seeking our own happiness or holiness more than the honor of God or the deliverance of men. Even where these are not entirely neglected, they do not always take the place they are meant to have. They must have the first place that makes everything, the dearest and best, secondary and subordinate to the work of helping and blessing men. The school of training for the priestly office is a reckless disregard of everything that would interfere with God's will and commands, a being jealous with God's jealousy against sin, and witnessing and fighting against it at any sacrifice.

We Need Men Of God!

This is what the world needs today. It needs men of God in whom the fire of God burns. It needs men who can stand, speak, and act in power on behalf of a God who, amid His own people, is dishonored by the worship of the golden calf. Understand that as you will. God often disapproves of a religion even where the people still profess to be in Covenant with God. "Consecrate yourselves today to the Lord, even every man upon his. . .brother" (Exodus 32:29). This call of Moses is also needed today. To each one who responds there is the reward of the priesthood.

All who want to fully know what the New Covenant means should remember God's Covenant of life and peace with Levi. Accept the holy calling to be an intercessor and burn incense before the Lord continually. Live, work, pray, and believe as one whom God has sought and found to stand in the gap before Him. The New Covenant was dedicated by a sacrifice and a death.

Consider this sacrifice as your most wonderful privilege and your fullest entrance into the Covenant life as you reflect the glory of the Lord and are changed into the same image from glory to glory. As you are led by the Spirit of the Lord, let the Spirit of that sacrifice and death be the moving power in all your priestly functions. Sacrifice yourself. Live and die for your fellow-men.

The Call To Intercessory Prayer

One of the great objects with which God has made a Covenant with us is to awaken strong confidence in Himself and His faithfulness to His promise. One of the objects that He has in waking and strengthening the faith in us is that He may use us as His channels of blessing to the world. In the work of saving men, He wants intercessory prayer to take the first place. He wants us to come to Him to receive, from Him in heaven, the spiritual life and power which can flow out from us to them.

He knows how difficult and hopeless it is in many cases to deal with sinners. He knows that it is no light thing for us to believe that in answer to our prayer the mighty power of God will move to save those around us. He knows that it needs strong faith to persevere patiently in prayer in cases in which the answer is long delayed and every year appears farther off than ever. So He undertakes, in our own experience, to prove what faith in His divine power can do. It brings down all the blessings of the New Covenant on us, that we may be able to confidently expect what we ask for others.

In our priestly life there is still another aspect.

The priests had no inheritance with their brethren. The Lord God was their inheritance. They had access to His dwelling and presence so that they might intercede there for others and then testify what God is and wills. Their personal privilege and experience prepared them for their work. If we want to intercede in power, we should live in the full realization of New Covenant life. It gives us more than liberty and confidence with God and the power to persevere. It also gives us power with men so we can testify to and prove what God has done to us. Here is the full glory of the New Covenant. Like Christ, its Mediator, we have the fire of divine love dwelling in us and consuming us in the service of men. The chief glory of the New Covenant to each of us should be that it is the Covenant of an everlasting priesthood.

Chapter 16

THE MINISTRY OF THE NEW COVENANT

"Ye are our epistle written in our hearts, known and read of all men: For as much as ye are manifest declared to be the epistle of Christ ministered by us, written not with ink, but with the Spirit of the living God; not in tables of stone, but in fleshly tables of the heart. And such trust have we through Christ God-ward: Not that we are sufficient of ourselves to think any thing as of ourselves; but our sufficiency is of God; Who also hath made us able ministers of the new testament; not of the letter, but of the Spirit: for the letter killeth, but the Spirit giveth life"—2 Corinthians 3:2-6.

We have seen that the New Covenant is a ministry of the Spirit which ministers all its grace and blessing in divine power and life. He does this through men who are called ministers of a New Covenant or ministers of the Spirit. The divine ministry of the Covenant to men and the earthly ministry of God's servants are equal in the power of the Holy Spirit. The ministry of the New Covenant has its glory and fruits in this. It is all to be a demonstration of the Spirit and of power.

What a contrast this is to the Old Covenant. Moses had received the glory of God shining upon him but had to put a veil over his face. Israel was incapable of looking at it. In hearing and reading Moses, there was a veil on their hearts. From Moses they could receive knowledge, thoughts, and desires. The power of God's Spirit to enable them to see the glory of what God speaks was not yet given.

Ministers Of The Spirit

This is the exceeding glory of the New Covenant. It is a ministry of the Spirit. Its ministers have their sufficiency from God, who makes them ministers of the Spirit and makes them able to speak the words of God in the Spirit. Then they are written in the heart, and the hearers become legible, living epistles of Christ showing the law written in their heart and life.

The ministry of the Spirit! What a glory there is in it! What a responsibility it brings! What a sufficiency of grace is provided for it! What a privilege to be a minister of the Spirit!

There are thousands throughout Christendom who are called ministers of the gospel. What an inconceivable influence they exert for life or death over the millions who depend upon them for their knowledge and participation of the Christian life. What a power there would be if all these were ministers of the Spirit! Let us study the Word until we see what God meant the ministry to be and learn to take our part in praying and laboring to have it nothing less.

God has made us ministers of the Spirit. The first thought is that a minister of the New Covenant must be a man personally possessed by the Holy Spirit. There is a twofold work of the Spirit. One, it gives a holy disposition and character. The other, it qualifies and empowers a man for work. The former must always come first. The promise of Christ to His disciples—that they should receive the Holy Spirit for their service—was very definitely given to those who had followed and loved Him and kept His commandments.

It is not enough that a man has been born of the Spirit. If he is to be a "sufficient minister" of the New Covenant, he must know what it is to be led by the Spirit, walk in the Spirit, and say, "The law of the Spirit of life in Christ Jesus hath made me free from the law of sin and death" (Romans 8:2). If you wanted to learn Greek or Hebrew would you accept a professor who hardly knows the elements of these languages?

How To Minister In The Spirit

How can a man be a minister of the New Covenant, which is so entirely "a ministry of the Spirit," unless he knows by experience what it is to live in the Spirit? The minister must, before everything, be a personal proof and witness of the truth and power of God in the fulfillment of what the New Covenant promises. Ministers are to be chosen men. They should be the best specimens and examples of what the Holy Spirit can do to sanctify a man, and by the working of God's power in him fit him for His service.

God has made us ministers of the Spirit. Next to this thought of being personally possessed by the Spirit comes the truth that all their work in the ministry can be done in the power of the Spirit. What an unspeakably precious assurance! Christ sends them to do a heavenly work—His work— and be instruments in His hands by which He works. He clothes them with a heavenly power. Their calling is to preach "the gospel unto you with the Holy Ghost sent down from heaven" (1 Peter 1:12). As far as feelings are concerned, they may have to say like Paul: "I was with you in weakness, and in fear, and in much trembling" (1 Corinthians 2:3). That does not prevent their adding, in fact, it may just be the secret of their being able to add, "My preaching was. . .in demonstration of the Spirit and of power" (1 Corinthians 2:4). If a man is to be a minister of the New Covenant, a messenger and a teacher of its true blessing to lead God's children to live in it, nothing less will do than a full experience of its power in himself, as the Spiritual ministers it.

Whether in his feeding on God's Word himself, his seeking in it for God's message for his people, in secret or intercessory prayer, or in private fellowship with souls or public teaching, he is to wait upon, receive, and yield to the energizing of the Holy Spirit. It is the mighty power of God working with him. This is his sufficiency for the work. Every day he may claim afresh and receive the anointing with fresh oil, the new inbreathing from Christ of His own Spirit and life.

God has made us ministers of the Spirit. There is still something that is no less important. The minister of the Spirit must especially see to it that *he lead men to the Holy Spirit.* Many will say, "If he is led of the Spirit in teaching men, is that not enough?" No. Men may become too dependent on him. They may take his Scripture teaching at second-hand. And, while there is power and blessing in his ministry, he may have reason to wonder why the results are not more definitely spiritual and permanent. The reason is simple.

The New Covenant is: "they shall not teach every man his. . . brother, saying, Know the Lord: for all shall know Me, from the least to the greatest" (Hebrews 8:11). The Father wants every child, from the least, to *live in continual, personal fellowship with Himself.* This cannot be, except as he is taught and helped to know and wait on the Holy Spirit. Bible study, prayer, faith, love, and obedience—the whole daily walk—must be taught as entirely dependent on the teaching and working of the indwelling Spirit.

Qualities Of A Minister

The minister of the Spirit definitely and perseveringly points away from himself to the Spirit. This is what John the Baptist did. He was filled with the Holy Spirit from his birth but sent men

124

away from himself to Christ, to be baptized by Him with the Spirit. Christ did the same. In His farewell discourse He called His disciples to turn from His personal instruction to the inward teaching of the Holy Spirit, who would dwell in them and guide them into the truth and power of all He had taught them.

Nothing is so needed in the Church today as this. All its feebleness, formalities, worldliness, lack of holiness, personal devotion to Christ, and enthusiasm for His cause and Kingdom is due to one thing. The Holy Spirit is not known, honored, and yielded to as the only, all-sufficient source of a holy life. The New Covenant is not known as a ministry of the Spirit in the heart of every believer. The one needful thing for the Church is the Holy Spirit in His power dwelling and ruling in the lives of God's saints.

One of the main ways to achieve this indwelling is for the ministers of the Spirit to live in the enjoyment and power of this great gift. They must persistently labor to bring their brethren into the possession of their birthright which is the Holy Spirit in the heart, maintaining, in divine power, an unceasing communion with the Son and the Father. The ministry of the Spirit makes the Spirit's ministry possible and effectual. The ministry of the Spirit again makes the ministration of the Spirit a reality in the life of the Church.

We know how dependent the Church is on its ministry. The converse is no less true. The ministers are dependent on the Church. They are its children. They breathe its atmosphere. They share its health or sickness. They are dependent upon its fellowship and intercession. None of us should think that all that the New Covenant calls us to is to see that we personally accept and rejoice in its blessings. No, God wants everyone who enters into it to know that its privileges are for all His children.

There is no more effectual way of doing this than thinking about the ministry of the Church. Compare the ministry around you with its pattern in God's Word (see especially 1 Corinthians 2; 2 Corinthians 3). Join with others who know how the New Covenant is nothing if it is not a ministration of the Spirit. Cry to God for a spiritual ministry. Ask the leading of God the Holy Spirit to teach you what can be done and what you can do to have the ministry of your Church become a truly spiritual one. Human condemnation will do as little good as human approval.

As the supreme place of the Holy Spirit, as the representative and revealer of the Father and Son is made clear to us, the one desire of our heart and our continual prayer will be that God would so reveal to all the ministers of His Word their heavenly calling. Then they may, above everything, seek this one thing—to be sufficient ministers of the New Covenant, not of the letter, but of the Spirit.

Chapter 17

HIS HOLY COVENANT

"To remember his Holy Covenant. . .grant unto us, that we being delivered out of the hand of our enemies might serve him without fear, in holiness and righteousness before him, all the days of our life"—Luke 1:72-75.

When Zacharias was filled with the Holy Spirit and prophesied, he spoke of God's visiting and redeeming His people as a remembering of His Holy Covenant. He speaks of the blessings of that Covenant, not in words that had been used before, but in what is manifestly a divine revelation to him by the Holy Spirit. He gathers up all the former promises in these words, "That we might serve Him without fear, *in holiness and righteousness before Him, all the days of our life.*" Holiness in life and service is to be the great gift of the Covenant of God's holiness. As we have seen before, the Old Covenant proclaimed and demanded holiness. The New provides it. Holiness of heart and life is its great gift.

God's Holiness

There is no attribute of God so difficult to define, so peculiarly a matter of divine revelation, so mysterious, incomprehensible, and inconceivably glorious, as His holiness. It is this holiness by which He is especially worshipped in His majesty on the throne of heaven (Isaiah 6:3; Revelation 4:8; Revelation 15:3-4). It unites His righteousness that judges and condemns with His love that saves and blesses. As the Holy One He is a consuming fire (Isaiah 10:17). As the Holy One He loves to dwell among His people (Isaiah 12:6). As the Holy One He is at an infinite distance from us. As the Holy One He comes inconceivably near and makes us one with and like Himself. The one purpose of His Holy Covenant is to make us holy as He is holy.

As the Holy One He says, "Be ye holy; for I am holy" (1 Peter 1:16); "I am the Lord which hallow you" (Leviticus 22:32). The highest conceivable summit of blessedness is our being partakers of the divine nature, of the divine holiness.

We Are Holy

This is the great blessing Christ, the Mediator of the New Covenant, brings. He has been made unto us "righteousness and sanctification"—righteousness as a preparation for sanctification or holiness (1 Corinthians 1:30). He prayed to the Father, "Sanctify them. . .for their sakes I *sanctify* Myself, that they also might be *sanctified* through the truth'' (John 17:17,19). Saints, in Him we are sanctified, holy ones (Romans 1:7; 1 Corinthians 1:2). We have put on the new man which is created after God in righteousnes and holiness. Holiness is our very nature.

We are holy in Christ. As we believe it, receive it, yield ourselves to the truth, and draw closer to God to have the holiness drawn forth and revealed in fellowship with Him, we will know how divinely true it is.

It is for this the Holy Spirit has been given in our hearts. He is the "Spirit of holiness." His every work is in the power of holiness. Paul says, "God hath from the beginning *chosen* you to salvation, *through sanctification of the Spirit* and belief of the truth" (2 Thessalonians 2:13). As simple and entire as our dependence on the Word of truth is, as the external means, our confidence must be in the hidden power for holiness which the working of the Spirit brings.

The connection between God's electing purpose and the working of the Spirit is clearly spoken of in Peter, *"Elect. . .through sanctification of the Spirit,* unto obedience" (1 Peter 1:2). The Holy Spirit is the Spirit of the life of Christ. As we know, honor, and trust Him, we will learn and experience that in the New Covenant the holiness of the Holy Spirit is our covenant right. We will be assured that, as God has promised, so He will work it in us, that we "might serve Him without fear, in righteousness and holiness before Him, all the days of our life." With a treasure of holiness in

Christ and the very Spirit of holiness in our hearts, we can live holy lives if we believe Him "who worketh in us both to will and to do of His good pleasure" (Philippians 2:13).

New Covenant Holiness

What new meaning is given to the teaching of the New Testament in the light of this Covenant promise. The Blessed Son and the Holy Spirit work it out in us. Take the first epistle Paul ever wrote. It was directed to men who only a few months previously had been turned from idols to serve the living God and wait for His Son from heaven. The words he speaks in regard to the holiness they might aim at and expect, because God was going to work it in them, are so grand that many Christians pass them by as practically unintelligible. "The Lord make you to increase and abound in love. . .to the end He *may stablish your hearts unblameable in holiness*. . .at the coming of our Lord Jesus Christ with all His saints" (1 Thessalonians 3:12-13). That promises unblameable holiness—and a heart unblameable in holiness—and we are established in all this by God Himself.

Paul might respond to the question, "Who hath believed our report?" with "Ye are witnesses. . .how *holily* and *justly* and *unblameably* we behaved ourselves" (1 Thessalonians 2:10). He assures them that what God has done for him, He will also do for them. He will give them hearts unblameable in holiness. The Church believes so little in the mighty power of God and the truth of

His Holy Covenant that the grace of such heart-holiness is hardly spoken of. The verse is often quoted in connection with "the coming of our Lord Jesus Christ with His saints," but its real point and glory is that when He comes, we may meet Him with *hearts stablished unblameable in holiness* by God Himself. This is not proclaimed or expected.

Take another verse in the epistle also spoken to these young converts in reference to the coming of our Lord. Some think that to speak much of the coming of the Lord will make us holy. How little it has done this in so many cases. It is the New Covenant holiness, worked in us by God Himself, believed in and waited for from Him, that can make our waiting differ from the carnal expectations of the Jews or the disciples.

Listen—"The very God of peace"—that is the keynote of the New Covenant—what you can never do, God will work in you. "Sanctify you wholly" this you may ask and expect—*"and I pray God your whole spirit and soul and body be preserved blameless unto the coming of our Lord Jesus Christ"* (1 Thessalonians 5:23). And now, as if to meet the doubt that will arise, *"Faithful is He that calleth you,* who will also do it" (1 Thessalonians 5:24). Again, it is the secret of the New Covenant—what has not entered into the heart of man—*God will work* in them that wait for Him. Until the Church awakes to see and believe that our holiness is to be the *immediate, almighty working of the Three-One God in us*

131

and that our *Christianity* must be an unceasing dependence to receive it *directly from Himself*, these promises remain a sealed book.

Now, let us return to the prophecy of the Holy Spirit by Zacharias, of God's remembering the Covenant of His Holiness, to make us holy, to establish our hearts unblameable in holiness that we should serve Him *in holiness and righteousness*. Note how every word is significant.

To grant us. It is to be a gift from above. The promise given with the Covenant was, "I the Lord have spoken it; *I will perform it."* We need to ask God to show us what *He will do*. When our faith expects all from Him, the blessing will be found.

That we being delivered out of the hands of our enemies. He had just said before, "*He hath raised up an horn of salvation for us. . .that we should be saved from our enemies, and from the hand of all that hate us"* (Luke 1:69, 71). Only free people can serve a holy God or be holy. It is only as the teaching of Romans 6-8 is experienced that I can expect God to do His mighty work in me. I need to know that I am "freed from sin;" "freed from the law;" and that "the Spirit of life in Christ Jesus hath made me free from the law of sin and death."

Might serve Him. My servant does not serve me by spending all his time getting himself ready for work but in doing work. The Holy Covenant sets us free and empowers us with divine grace so that God can have us for His work. It is the same work Christ began, and we now carry on.

Without fear. We must have childlike confidence and boldness before God and men. It is freedom from fear in every difficulty, because we have learned that God works all in us so we can trust Him to work all for us and through us.

Before Him. We have His continued, unceasing presence all day as the unceasing security of our obedience and fearlessness. It is the never failing secret of our being sanctified wholly.

All our days. Not only all the day for one day, but for every day, because Jesus is a High Priest in the power of an endless life. The mighty operation of God as promised in the Covenant is as unchanging as God is Himself.

Can you not begin to see that God's Word appears to mean more than you have ever conceived of or expected? It is only when you begin to say, *Glory to Him* who is able to do *exceeding abundantly above all* we can ask or think that you will really come to the place of helplessness and dependence where God can work. You must expect God's almighty, supernatural, altogether immeasurable power and grace to work out the New Covenant life in you and *make you holy*.

Brethren, believe that God's Word is true, and say with Zacharias, "Blessed be the Lord God of Israel, for He hath visited and redeemed His people. . .to remember His Holy Covenant grant unto us, that we being delivered out of the hand of our enemies might serve Him without fear, *in holiness and righteousness before Him all the days of our life*" (Luke 1:68,72-75).

133

Chapter 18

ENTERING THE COVENANT WITH ALL THE HEART

"And they entered into a covenant to seek the Lord God of their fathers with all their heart and with all their soul"—2 Chronicles 15:12.

"The Lord thy God will circumcise thine heart, and the heart of thy seed, to love the Lord thy God with all thine heart, and with all thy soul"—Deuteronomy 30:6.

"And I will give them an heart to know me, that I am the Lord: and they shall be my people, and I will be their God: for they shall return unto me with their whole heart"—Jeremiah 24:7.

"I will make an everlasting covenant with them, that I will not turn away from them, to do them good; but I will put my fear in their hearts, that they shall not depart from me. Yea, I will rejoice over them to do them good. . .with my whole heart and my whole soul"—Jeremiah 32:40-41.

In the days of Asa, Hezekiah, and Josiah we read

about Israel entering into "the Covenant" with their whole heart, "to perform the words of this Covenant that were written in this book" (2 Kings 23:3). Of Asa's day we read, "They swear unto the Lord. . .and all Judah rejoiced at the oath: for they had sworn with all their *heart,* and sought Him with their whole *desire;* and He was found of them" (2 Chronicles 15:14,15). Wholehearted- ness is the secret of our entering the Covenant and finding God in it. Wholeheartedness is the secret of joy in Christianity—a full entrance into all the blessedness the Covenant brings. God rejoices over His people to do them good, *with His whole heart and His whole soul.* We need *our whole heart and our whole soul* to enter into and enjoy this joy of God in doing us good with His whole heart and His whole soul. With what measure we mete, it will be measured unto us again.

Love God With All Your Heart

If we have at all understood the teaching of God's Word in regard to the New Covenant, we know what it reveals about the two parties who meet in it. On God's side there is the promise to do for us and in us all that we need to serve and enjoy Him. He will rejoice in doing us good, with His whole heart. He will be our God, doing for us all that a God can do, giving Himself as God to be wholly ours. On our side there is the prospect of our being able, in the power of what He engages to do, to "return unto Him with our whole heart," "to love Him with all our heart and all our

135

strength.''

The first and great commandment, the only possible terms on which God can fully reveal Himself or give Himself to His creature to enjoy, is, "Thou shalt love the Lord thy God with all thy heart" (Matthew 22:37). That law is unchangeable. The New Covenant comes and brings us the grace to obey by lifting us into the love of God. It calls upon us in the faith of that grace to rise and be of good courage. With our whole heart we must yield ourselves to the God of the Covenant and life in His service.

Wholeheartedness in the love and service of God! How should I speak of it and its imperative necessity? It is the one unalterable condition of true communion with God, of which nothing can supply the need. How can I speak of its infinite reasonableness? Such a God, who is the very Fountain of all that is loving and lovely, of all that is good and blessed, the All-glorious God. Surely there cannot for a moment be a thought of anything else being His due or of our consenting to offer Him anything less than the love of the whole heart. How can I speak of its unspeakable blessedness? To love Him with the whole heart is the only possible way of receiving His great love into our heart and rejoicing in it. We must yield ourselves to that great love and allow God Himself, just as an earthly love enters into us and makes us glad, to give us the taste and joy of the heavenliness of that love.

How can I speak of its terrible lack? Where will

I find words to open the eyes and reach the heart? How can I show how almost universal the lack of true wholeheartedness in the faith and love of God is? It is lacking in our seeking to love Him with the whole heart and in our giving up everything to possess Him, please Him, and be wholly possessed of Him.

The Certainty Of Wholeheartedness

And then what of the blessed certainty of its attainableness? The Covenant has provided for it. The Triune God will work it by taking possession of the heart and dwelling there. The blessed Mediator of the Covenant undertakes for all we have to do. His constraining love shed abroad in our hearts by the Holy Spirit can bring and maintain it. Yes, how will I speak of all this?

Have we not said enough already? We need something more than words and thoughts. What we need is to quietly turn to the Holy Spirit who dwells in us. With faith in the light and strength our Lord gives through Him, we need to accept and act out what God tells about the heart He has placed within us. We must yield to the wholeheartedness He works. Surely the new heart given to us to love God with, and which has God's Spirit in it, is wholly for God. Let our faith accept and rejoice in the wondrous gift and not be afraid to say, "I will love Thee, O Lord, with my whole heart." Just think for a moment what it means that God has given us such a heart.

We know what God's giving means. *His giving*

depends on our taking . He does not force spiritual possessions on us. He promises and gives in such measure as desire and faith are ready to receive. He gives in divine power. As faith trusts and yields itself to that power, the gift becomes consciously and wholly our possession.

God's spiritual gifts *are not recognized by sense or reason.* "Eye hath not seen, nor ear heard, neither have entered into the heart of man, *the things which God hath prepared* for them that love Him. But God hath *revealed them unto us by His Spirit.* . . .Now we have received. . .the Spirit which is of God; that we might *know the things that are freely given to us of God"* (1 Corinthians 2:9-10,12). It is as you yield yourself to be led and taught by the Spirit that your faith will be able, despite all lack of feeling, to rejoice in the possession of the new heart and all that is given with it.

Then, *this divine giving is continuous.* I bestow a gift on a man. He takes it, and I never see him again. So God gives temporal gifts to men, and they never think of Him. But, spiritual gifts are only to be received and enjoyed in unceasing communication with God Himself. The new heart is not a power I have in myself, like the natural endowments of thinking or loving. No, it is only in unceasing dependence on and close contact with God that the heavenly gift of a new heart can be maintained uninjured and day by day become stronger. It is only in God's immediate presence and in unceasing, direct dependence on Him that

138

spiritual endowments are preserved.

Then, further, *spiritual gifts can only be enjoyed by acting them out in faith*. None of the graces of the Christian life—like love, meekness, or boldness—can be felt or known, much less strengthened, until we begin to exercise them. We must not wait to feel them or feel the strength for them. We must practice them in the obedience of the faith that they are given and hidden within us. Whatever we read of the new heart and of all God has given into it in the New Covenant must be boldly believed and carried out in action.

All this is especially true of wholeheartedness and loving God with all our heart. You may at first be very ignorant of all it implies. God has planted the new heart in the midst of the flesh. The animating principle, of the flesh—*self*—has to be denied, kept crucified, and be mortified by the Holy Spirit. God has placed you in the midst of a world from which you are to come out and be entirely separate. God has given you your work in His Kingdom, for which He asks all your interest, time, and strength.

Give God Your Whole Heart

In all these three respects you need wholeheartedness to enable you to make the sacrifices that may be required. If you take the ordinary standard of Christian life around you, you will find that wholeheartedness and intense devotion to God and His service are hardly thought of. How to make the best of both worlds, innocently to enjoy

139

as much as possible of this present life, is the ruling principle. As a natural consequence, the present world secures the larger share of interest. To please self is considered legitimate, and the Christlike life of *not pleasing self* has little place. Wholeheartedness will lead and enable you to accept Christ's command and sell all for the pearl of great price. At first you may be afraid of what it may involve. Do not hesitate to speak the word frequently in the ear of your Father, *with my whole heart*. You may count on the Holy Spirit to open up its meaning, show you to what service or sacrifice God calls you in it, increase its power, reveal its blessedness, and make it the very spirit of your life of devotion to your Covenant God.

And now, who is ready to enter into this new and everlasting Covenant with his whole heart? Each of us should do it.

Begin very humbly by asking God to give you, by the Spirit who dwells in you, the vision of the heavenly life and wholehearted love and obedience as it has actually been prepared for you in Christ. It is an existing reality, a spiritual endowment out of the life of God which can come upon you. It is secured for you in the Covenant and in Christ Jesus, its Surety. Ask earnestly, definitely, believingly, that God will reveal this to you. Do not rest until you know fully what your Father means you to be and has provided for your being.

When you begin to see why the New Covenant was given, what it promises, and how divinely certain its promises are, *offer yourself to God unre-*

servedly to be taken up into it. If He will take you in, offer to love Him with your whole heart and obey Him with all your strength. Do not hold back or be afraid.

God has sworn to do you good *with His whole heart*. Do not hesitate to say that you now wholeheartedly enter into this Covenant in which *He promises to cause you* to turn to Him and love Him with your whole heart. If there is any fear, just ask again believing for a vision of the Covenant life. God swears to do you good with *His whole heart*. He undertakes to make and enable you to love and obey Him with *your whole heart*. The vision of this life will make you bold to say: Into this Covenant of a wholehearted love in God and in me I now enter with my whole heart.

Let us close with this one thought. A redeeming God, rejoicing with His whole heart and soul to do us good and work in us all that is well-pleasing in His sight, this is the one side. This is the God of the Covenant. Look at Him. Believe Him. Worship Him. Wait on Him until the fire begins to burn and your heart is drawn out with all its might to love this God. Then there is the other side. A redeemed soul, rejoicing with all its heart and soul in the love of this God, entering into the covenant of wholehearted love and venturing to say to Him, "With my whole heart I do love You, God, my exceeding joy." These are the children of the Covenant.

Reader, do not rest until you have entered in, through the beautiful gate, through Christ the door, into this temple of love—the heart of God.

NOTES

Note A

THE SECOND BLESSING

In the life of the believer there sometimes comes a crisis, as clearly marked as his conversion, in which he passes out of a life of continual feebleness and failure into one of strength, victory, and abiding rest. The transition has been called the Second Blessing. Many have objected to the phrase because they think it is unscriptural or tends to make a general rule for everyone when it was only a method of experience in some.

Others have used it to help clearly express in human words what ought to be taught to believers as a possible deliverance from the ordinary life of the Christian, to one of abiding fellowship with God and entire devotion to His service. In introducing it into the title of this book, I have indicated my belief that the words express a scriptural truth and may help believers in clearly putting before them what they can expect from God. Let me try to clarify how I think we ought to understand it.

Victory Over Sin

I have connected the expression with the two Covenants. Why did God make two Covenants—not one or three? Because there were two parties concerned. In the First Covenant man was to prove what he could do and what he was. In the Second, God would show what He would do. The former was the time of needed preparation. The latter was the time of divine fulfillment. The same necessity as there was for this in the whole of mankind exists in the individual, too.

Conversion makes a sinner a child of God, full of ignorance and weakness, without any conception of what the wholehearted devotion that God asks of him is or the full possession God is ready to take of him. In some cases the transition from the elementary stage is by a gradual growth and enlightenment. But, experience teaches that in the great majority of cases this healthy growth is not found.

To those who have never found the secret of victory over sin and perfect rest in God and have despaired of ever finding it because of their failure, it has often been a wonderful help to learn that by a single, decisive step, they can have a right relationship to Christ, His Spirit, and His strength. It is possible to enter into an entirely new life.

Confess Your Sin

What is needed to help a man to take that step is

very simple. He must see and confess the sin of the life he is living which is not in harmony with God's will. He must see and believe in the life which Scripture holds out and which Christ Jesus promises to work and maintain in him. As he sees that his failure has been due to his striving in his own strength and believes that our Lord Jesus will actually work all in him in divine power, he takes courage and dares to surrender himself to Christ anew.

Confessing and giving up all that is of self and sin and yielding himself wholly to Christ and His service, he believes and receives a new power to live his life by the faith of the Son of God. The change is in many cases as clear, marked, and as wonderful as conversion. For lack of a better name, that of *A Second Blessing* came most naturally.

Once we see how greatly this change is needed in the life of most Christians and how entirely it rests on faith in Christ and His power as revealed in the Word, all doubt of its scripturalness will be removed. Once its truth is seen, we will be surprised to find how throughout Scripture and in history and teaching we find what illustrates and confirms it.

Take the twofold passage of Israel through water, first out of Egypt and then into Canaan. The wilderness journey was the result of unbelief and disobedience. It was allowed by God to humble, prove, and show them what was in their heart. When this purpose had been accomplished, a second blessing led them through Jordan, as mightily into Canaan as the first had brought them through the Red Sea out of Egypt.

Or, take the Holy Place and the Holiest of All as types of life in the two covenants and equally in the two stages of Christian experience. In the former there is very real access to God and fellowship with Him, but it is always with a veil between. In the latter there is the full access into the immediate presence of God and the full experience of the power of the heavenly life. As the eyes are opened to see how terribly the average Christian life falls short of God's purpose and how truly the mingled life can be expelled by the power of a new revelation of what God waits to do, the verses of Scripture will shine with new meaning.

Surrender To The Spirit

Look at the teachings of the New Testament. In Romans, Paul contrasts the life of the Christian under the law with that under grace—the spirit of bondage with the Spirit of adoption. What does this mean but that Christians may still live under the law and its bondage. They need to come out of this into the full life of grace and liberty through the Holy Spirit. When they first see the difference, nothing is needed but the surrender of faith to accept and experience what grace will do by the Holy Spirit. Paul writes to the Corinthians of some being carnal and still babes walking as men after the flesh. Others are spiritual, with spiritual discernment and character. To the Galatians, he speaks of the liberty with which Christ, by the Spirit, makes free from the law. He contrasts this with those who sought to perfect in the flesh what was begun in the Spirit and who gloried in the flesh. All these teachings call believers to recognize the danger of the carnal, divided life and to come at once to the life of faith, the life in the Spirit, which alone is according to God's will.

How sad that the Church of the present day often makes the same mistakes about living a carnal, divided life. Conversion is only the gate that leads into the path of life. Within that gate there is still great danger of mistaking the path, turning aside, or turning back. Where this has taken place we are called at once with our whole heart to turn and give ourselves to nothing less than all that Christ is willing to work in us.

There are many who have always thought that conversion must be slow, gradual, and uncertain because they only take man's powers into account and cannot understand how it can be sudden and final. Many fail to see how the revelation of the true life of holiness and the entrance into it by faith out of a life of self-effort and failure can be immediate and permanent. They look at man's efforts too much and do not know how the Second Blessing is nothing more nor less than a new vision of what Christ is willing to work in us. It is the surrender of faith that yields all to Him.

I hope that what I have written in this book may help some to see that the Second Blessing is just what they need. It is what God by His Spirit will work in them. It is nothing but the acceptance of Christ in all His saving power as our strength and life. It will bring them into and prepare them for that full life in the New Covenant in which God works all in all.

Let me close this note with a quotation from the introduction to the book *Dying to Self: A Golden Dialogue* by William Law. "A great deal has been said against the use of the terms, the Higher Life, the Second Blessing. In Law one finds nothing of such language, but of the deep truth of which they are the, perhaps defective, expression this book is full of. The points on which so much stress is laid in what is called Keswick teaching stand prominently out in his whole argument. The following truths are common to both: the low state of the average life of believers, the cause of all failure as coming from self-confidence, the need of an entire surrender of the whole being to the operation of God, the call to turn to Christ as the One and Sure Deliverer from the power of self, the divine certainty of a better life for all who will in self-despair trust Christ for it, and the heavenly joy of a life in which the Spirit of love fills the heart. What makes Law's putting of the truth of special value is the way in which he shows how humility and utter self-despair, with the resignation to God's mighty working in simple faith, is the infallible way to be delivered from self, and have the Spirit of Love fill the heart."

THE LAW WRITTEN IN THE HEART

The thought of the law written in the heart sometimes causes difficulty and discouragement, because believers do not see or feel anything corresponding to it. An illustration may help this difficulty. There are fluids you can write with so that nothing is visible, either at once or later, unless the writing is exposed to the sun or the action of some chemical. The writing is there, but the person who is ignorant of the process cannot believe it is there and does not know how to make it readable. The man of faith who knows of the process realizes it is there even though he does not see it.

The Lord In The Heart

It is also true with the new heart. God has put His law into it. "Blessed are the people in whose heart is God's law." But, it is there invisibly. He takes God's promise in faith and knows that it is in his own heart. As long as there is no clear faith on this point, all attempts to find it or fulfill that law

151

will be vain. But when by simple faith the promise is held fast, the first step is taken to realize it. The soul is then prepared to receive instruction as to what the writing of the law in the heart means.

First, it means that God has implanted in the new heart a love of God's law and a readiness to do all His will. You may not feel this dispositon there, but it is there. God has put it there. Believe this and be assured that there is a divine nature in you which says—and therefore you do not hesitate to say it—"I delight to do Thy will, O my God" (Psalm 40:8). In the name of God, and in faith, say it.

This writing of the law also means that in planting this principle in you, God has taken all that you know of God's will already and inspired that new heart with the readiness to obey it. It may be written there with invisible writing, and you are not conscious of it. That does not matter. Here you have to deal with a divine and hidden work of the Holy Spirit. Do not be afraid to say, "Oh, how I love Your law!" God has put the love of it into your new heart. He has taken away the stony heart. You have to live by the new heart.

The next thing implied in this writing of the law is that you have accepted all God's will, even what you do not know yet as the delight of your heart. In giving yourself up to God, you gave yourself wholly to His will. That was the one condition to your entering the Covenant. Covenant grace will now teach you to know and strengthen you to do all your Father would have you do.

We Need More Faith

The entire life in the New Covenant is a life of faith. Faith accepts every promise of the Covenant, is certain that it is being fulfilled, and looks confidently to the God of the Covenant to do His work. Faith believes implicitly in the new heart with the law written in it because it believes in the promise and in the God who gave and fulfills the promise.

It may be well to add here that the same truth holds true of all the promises concerning the new heart. They must be accepted and acted on by faith. When we read "the love of God is shed abroad in our hearts by the Holy Ghost," "Christ may dwell in your hearts," "a clean heart," "love one another with a pure heart fervently," and "God stablish your hearts unblameable in holiness," we must, with the eye of faith, regard these spiritual realities as actually existing within us (Romans 5:5; Ephesians 3:17; 1 Peter 1:22; 1 Thessalonians 3:13).

In His hidden, unseen way God is working them there. We know—not by sight or feeling but by faith in the living God and His Word—that they are an inspiration for the dispositions and inclinations of the new heart. We are to act in this faith knowing that we have the power to love, obey, and be holy. The New Covenant gives us a God who works all in us. Faith in Him gives us the assurance above and beyond all feeling that God is doing His blessed work. If we ask what we are to think of all there is within us that contradicts this faith, let us remember what Scripture teaches. We sometimes speak of an old and new heart. Scripture does not do this. It speaks of the old, stony heart being taken away. The heart, with its will, disposition, and affections, is being made new with a divine newness. This new heart is placed in the midst of what Scripture calls the flesh, where "no good thing dwells."

We will find it a great advantage to adhere as closely as possible to Scripture language. It will help our faith greatly to use the very words God, by His Holy Spirit, uses to teach us. It will also clear our view for knowing what to think of the sin that remains in us if we think of it and deal with it in the light of God's truth. Every evil desire and affection comes from the flesh, man's sinful natural life. It owes its power to our ignorance of its nature and our trusting to its help and strength to cast out its evil. I have already pointed out how sinful flesh and religious flesh are one and how all failure in our Christian walk is due to a secret trust in ourselves.

Renounce The Flesh

As we accept and make use of what God says of the flesh, we will realize that it is the source of all evil in us. We will say of its temptations, "It is no more I, but sin that dwells in me." We will maintain our integrity as we maintain a good conscience that condemns us for nothing knowingly done against God's will. We will be strong in the faith of the Holy Spirit, who dwells in the new heart to strengthen us so that we "will not fulfill the lusts of the flesh."

I conclude with a paraphrase of an address by Rev. F. Webster, a respected Keswick speaker, in confirmation of what I have just said. "Put on the Lord Jesus Christ, and do not make provision for the flesh, to fulfill the lusts thereof. 'Make not provision for the flesh' (Romans 13:14). The flesh is there. To deny or ignore the existence of an enemy is to give him a great chance against you. The flesh is in the believer to the very end. It is a force of evil to be reckoned with continually. It is an evil force inside a man, and yet, thank God, a force which can be so dealt with by the power of God that it will have no power to defile the heart or deflect the will. The flesh is in you, but your heart may be kept clean moment by moment in spite of the existence of evil in your fallen nature. Every avenue, every opening that leads into the heart, and every thought, desire, purpose, and imagination of your being may be closed against the flesh so that there will be no opening to come in and defile the heart or deflect the will from the will of God.

"You say that is a very high standard, but it is the Word of God. There is to be no secret sympathy with sin. Although the flesh is there, you are to make it no excuse for sins. You are not to say, I am naturally irritable, anxious, jealous, and I cannot help letting these things crop up. They come from within. Yes, they come from within, but there does not have to be any provision or opening in your heart for these things to enter. Your heart can be barricaded with an impassable barrier against these things. 'Make not provision for the flesh' (Romans 13:14). Not only should the front door be barred and bolted so that you do not invite them to come in, but the side and back door should be closed, too. You can be so Christ-possessed and Christ-enclosed that you will positively hate everything that is of the flesh.

" 'Make not provision for the flesh' (Romans 13:14). The only way to do this is to 'put ye on the Lord Jesus Christ' (Romans 13:14). I spoke of the heart being so barricaded that there could be no entrance to it. The flesh should never be able to defile it or deflect the will from the will of God. How can that be done? By putting on the Lord Jesus Christ. It has been such a blessing to me just to learn that one secret, the positive side of deliverance—putting on the Lord Jesus Christ."

Note C

GEORGE MUELLER AND HIS SECOND CONVERSION

In the life of George Mueller of Bristol there was an epoch, four years after his conversion, which he often spoke about as his entrance into the true Christian life.

Full Surrender

In an address given to ministers and workers after his ninetieth birthday, he spoke the following of it himself. "That leads to another thought— the full surrender of the heart to God. I *was converted* in November, 1825, but I only *came into the full surrender of the heart* four years later in July, 1829. The love of money, the love of place, the love of position, the love of worldly pleasures and engagements were gone. God alone became my portion. I found my all in Him; I wanted nothing else. And, by the grace of God this has remained and has made me an exceedingly happy man. It led me to care only about the things of God. I ask affectionately, brethren, have you fully surrendered your heart to God or is there this or that thing with which you are taken up irrespective of God? I read a little of the Scriptures before but preferred other books. Since that time the revelation He has made of Himself has become unspeakably blessed to me, and I can say from my heart, God is an infinitely lovely Being. Oh! Do not be satisfied until in your inmost soul you can say, God is an infinitely lovely Being!"

The account he gives of this change in his journal is as follows. He speaks of one whom he had heard preach at Teignmouth where he had gone for the sake of his health. "Though I did not like all he said, I saw a gravity and solemnity in him different from the rest. Through the instrumentality of this brother the Lord gave me a great blessing which I will thank Him for throughout eternity.

"God then began to show me that the Word of God alone is to be our standard of judgment in spiritual things. It can only be explained by the Holy Spirit. In our day as well as in former times, He is the Teacher of His people. *I had not experimentally understood the office of the Holy Spirit before that time*. Before I had not seen that the Holy Spirit alone can teach us about our state by nature, show us our need of a Savior, enable us to believe in Christ, explain to us the Scriptures, help us in preaching, etc.

"It was my beginning to understand this point in particular which had a great effect on me. The Lord enabled me to put it to the test of experience

158

by laying aside commentaries and almost every other book and simply reading the Word of God and studying it. The result was that the first evening I shut myself into my room to give myself to prayer and meditation over the Scriptures, I learned more in a few hours than I had previously done during a period of several months. *But the particular difference was that I received real strength in my soul in doing so*.

"In addition to this, it pleased the Lord to lead me to see a *higher standard of devotedness* than I had seen before. He led me, in a measure, to see what is my glory in this world, even to be despised, poor, and mean with Christk. . .I returned to London much better in body. And in regard to my soul, *the change was so great that it was like a second conversion.*"

The Word Is Essential Reading

In another passage he says, "I fell into the snare which so many young believers fall into. The reading of religious books is preferred to the Scriptures. Now the Scriptural way of reasoning would have been this. God Himself has condescended to become an author, and I am ignorant of that precious Book which His Holy Spirit has caused to be written. Therefore I ought to read this Book of books again very earnestly, prayerfully, and with much meditation.

"Instead of acting this way and being led by my ignorance of the Word to study it more, my difficulty of understanding it made me careless of reading it. Then, like many believers, I practically preferred the works of uninspired men for the first four years of my Christian life to the oracles of the Living God. The consequence was that I remained a babe both in knowledge and grace. I say in knowledge for all true knowledge must be derived by the Spirit from the Word. This lack of knowledge kept me back from walking steadily in the ways of God.

"It is the truth that makes us free by delivering us from the slavery of the lusts of the flesh, the lusts of the eyes, and the pride of life. The Word, the experience of the saints, and also my own experience most decidedly proves it. For when it pleased the Lord in August, 1829 to bring me really to the Scriptures, my life and walk became very different.

"If any one would ask me how he may read the Scriptures most profitably, I would answer him:

"1. Above all he must seek to have it settled in his own mind *that God alone, by the Holy Spirit, can teach him*. Therefore, since God will be sought for all blessings, it becomes him to seek God's blessing prior to reading, and also while reading.

"2. He should also have it settled in his mind that though *the Holy Spirit is the best and sufficient Teacher*, yet He does not always teach immediately when we desire it. Therefore, *we may have to ask Him again and again* for the explanation of certain passages. But *He will surely teach us* if we will seek for light prayerfully, patiently, and for the glory of God."

Let us look at one more passage from an address given on his ninetieth birthday. "For sixty-nine years and ten months he had been a very happy man. He attributed that to two things. He had maintained a good conscience, not willfully going on in a course he knew to be contrary to the mind of God. He did not, of course, mean that he was perfect. He was poor, weak, and sinful. Secondly, he attributed it to his love of Holy Scripture. Lately his practice had been to read through the Scriptures four times every year with meditation and application to his own heart. That day he was a greater lover of God's Word than he was sixty-six years ago. It was this and maintaining a good conscience that had given him peace and joy in the Holy Ghost all these years."

The Spirit Brings Power

In connection with what has been said about the New Covenant being a work of the Spirit, this narrative is most helpful. It shows us how George Mueller's power lay in God's revealing to him the work of the Holy Spirit. He writes that up to the time of that change he had "Not experimentally understood the office of the Holy Spirit." We speak much of George Mueller's power in prayer. It is important to remember that that power was entirely due to his love of and faith in God's Word.

But, it is still more important to notice that his power to believe God's Word so fully was entirely due to his having learned to know the Holy Spirit as his Teacher. When the words of God are explained to us and made living within us by the Holy Spirit, they have a power to awaken faith which they otherwise have not. The Word then brings us into contact with God, comes to us directly from God, and binds our whole life to Him.

When the Holy Spirit feeds us on the Word, our whole life comes under His power and the fruit is seen not only in the power of prayer but in the power of obedience. Notice how Mr. Mueller tells us this. The two secrets of his great happiness were his great love for God's Word and his *ever maintaining a good conscience*, not knowingly doing anything against the will of God. In giving himself to the teaching of the Holy Spirit, he made a full surrender of his entire heart to God to be ruled by the Word. He gave himself to obey that Word in everything.

He believed that the Holy Spirit gave the grace to obey, and so he was able to maintain a walk free from knowingly transgressing God's law. This is a point he always insisted on. He writes the following in regard to a life of dependence upon God. "It will not do—it is not possible—*to live in sin* and at the same time, by communion with God, to draw down from heaven everything one needs for the life that now is."

Again, speaking of the strengthening of faith he says, "It is of the utmost importance that we seek to maintain *an upright heart and a good conscience*. Therefore do not knowingly and habitually indulge in those things which are contrary to the mind of God. All my confidence in God, all my leaning upon Him in the hour of trial, will be gone if I have a guilty conscience, and do not seek to put away this guilty conscience, but still continue to do things which are contrary to His mind."

A careful reading of this testimony will show us how the chief points insisted upon in connection with the second blessing are all found here. There is a full surrender of the heart to be taught and led alone by the Spirit of God. There is the higher standard of holiness which is set up at once. There is the tender desire to offend God in nothing but to have a good conscience at all times that testifies that we are pleasing to God. And, there is the faith that where the Holy Spirit reveals the will of God to us in the Word, He gives sufficient strength for doing it. "The particular difference," he says about reading with faith in the Holy Spirit's teaching, "was that I received real strength in my soul in doing so."

Everything centers in this, that we believe in the New Covenant and its promises as a work of the Spirit. That belief may come suddenly to some, as it did to George Mueller. Or, it may dawn upon others by degrees. All must say to God that they are ready to put their whole heart and life under the rule of the Holy Spirit dwelling in them, teaching them by the Word, and strengthening them by His grace. He enables us to live pleasing to God.

Note D

CANON BATTERSBY

I do not know whether I can find a better illustration of the place Christ, the Mediator of the Covenant, takes in leading into its full blessing than that of the founder of the Keswick Convention, the late Canon Battersby.

It was at the Oxford Convention in 1873 that he witnessed to having "received a new and distinct blessing to which he had been a stranger before." For more than twenty-five years he had been very diligent as a minister of the gospel and, from his journals, most faithful in seeking to maintain a close walk with God. But, he was always disturbed by the consciousness of being overcome by sin. As far back as 1853 he had written, "I feel again how very far I am from habitually enjoying that peace, love, and joy which Christ promises. I must confess that I do not have it, and that very ungentle, unchristian tempers often strive within me for the mastery."

The Rest Of Faith

In 1873 when he read what was being published of the Higher Life, the effect made him utterly dissatisfied with himself and his state. There were difficulties he could not quite understand in that teaching. But, he felt that he must either reach forward to better things, nothing less than redemption from *all* iniquities, or fall back more and more into worldliness and sin. At Oxford he heard an address on the rest of faith. It opened his eyes to the truth that a believer who really longs for deliverance from sin must simply take Christ at His word. He must believe, without feeling, on Him to do His work of cleansing and keeping the soul.

"I thought of the sufficiency of Jesus, and said, 'I *will rest* in Him,' and I did rest in Him. I was afraid that it would be a passing emotion. But, I found that a presence of Jesus was graciously manifested to me in a way I did not know before, and that *I did abide in Him*. I do not want to rest in these emotions, but just believe and cling to Christ as my all." He was a man with a very reserved nature, but he felt it his duty before the close of the Conference to publicly confess his past shortcoming and openly testify to his having entered upon a new and definite experience.

In a paper written not long after this he explained the steps that led to this experience. *First*, there is a clear view of the possibilities of Christian attainment—a life in word and action, habitually governed by the Spirit, in constant communion with God, and continual victory over sin through abiding in Christ. *Then*, there must be the deliberate purpose of the will for a full renunciation of all the idols of the flesh or spirit and a will-surrender to Christ. Then comes this last and important step. *We must look up to and wait on our ascended Lord for all we need to enable us to do this*.

Faith Centers In Christ

A careful reading of this very brief statement will prove how everything centers in Christ. The surrender for a life of continual communion and victory is to be given up to Christ. The strength for that life is to be in Him and from Him by faith in Him. And *the power* to make the full surrender and rest in Him *is to be waited for* from *Him alone*.

In June, 1875, the first Keswick Convention was held. In the newspaper reporting it we read, "Many everywhere are thirsting that they may be brought to enjoy more of the divine presence in their daily life, and a fuller manifestation of the Holy Spirit's power, whether in subduing the lusts of the flesh or in enabling them to offer more effective service to God. It is certainly God's will that His children should be satisfied in regard to these longings. There are those who can testify that He has satisfied them and does satisfy them with daily fresh manifestations of His grace and power."

The results of the very first Convention were so

blessed that after its close he wrote, "There is a very remarkable resemblance in the testimonies I have since received as to the nature of the blessing obtained, and *the ability given* to make a full surrender to the Lord and the consequent experience of an abiding peace far exceeding anything previously experienced." Through all, the chief thought was Christ first drawing and enabling the soul to rest in Him, and then meeting it with the fulfillment of its desire—the abiding experience of His power to keep it in victory over sin and in communion with God.

What was the fruit of this new experience? Eight years later Cánon Battersby spoke, "it is now eight years since I knew this blessing as my own. I cannot say that I have never for a moment ceased to trust the Lord to keep me. But I can say that as long as I have trusted Him, He has kept me. He has been faithful."

Note E

NOTHING OF MYSELF

One would think that no words could make it plainer than the words of the Covenant state—that the one difference between Old and New is that in the latter everything is to be done by God Himself. Yet believers and even teachers do not take it in. Even those who do understand it find it difficult to live it out. Our whole being is so blinded to the true relationship to God. His inconceivable, omnipresent omnipotence working in us every moment is so far beyond the reach of human conception, our little hearts cannot rise to the reality of His infinite love making itself one with us. We fail to conceive how He delights to dwell in us and to work all in us that has to be done there. When we think we have accepted the truth, we find it is only a thought. We are such strangers to the knowledge of what *a God* really is, as the actual life by which His creatures live. *In Him* we live and move and have our being.

And, the knowledge of the Triune God is especially too high for us. It is beyond our comprehension to understand that wonderful, most real, and most practical indwelling which enabled the Son to become Incarnate and the Holy Spirit to be sent into our hearts. Only they who confess their ignorance and wait very humbly and persistently on our blessed God to teach us by His Holy Spirit what that all-working indwelling is can hope to have it revealed to them.

Christ Depends On The Father

In preparing a series of Bible lessons for our Students Association here, I made a study of the gospel of John and the life of our Lord which is set forth there. I cannot say how deeply I have been impressed with the profound secret of His life on earth—*His dependence on the Father*. It has come to me like a new revelation. Twelve times or more He uses the word *not* and *nothing* of Himself. *Not* My will. *Not* My words. *Not* My honor. *Not* Mine own glory. I can do *nothing* of Myself. I speak *not* of Myself. I came *not* of Myself. I do *nothing* of Myself.

Just think a moment what this means in connection with what He tells us of His life in the Father. "As the Father hath life in Himself; so hath He given to the Son to have life in Himself" (John 5:26). "That all men should honour the Son, even as they honour the Father" (John 5:23). And yet this Son, who has life in Himself even as the Father has, immediately adds: "I can of Mine own self do *nothing*" (John 5:30). We should have thought that with this life in Himself He would have the

169

power of independent action as the Father has. But no. "The Son can do *nothing* of Himself, but what He seeth the Father do" (John 5:19).

The chief mark of this divine life He has in Himself is evidently unceasing dependence, continually receiving from the Father what He had to speak or do. *Nothing of Myself* is manifestly as true of Him as it ever could be of the weakest or most sinful man. The life of the Father dwelling in Christ, and Christ in the Father, meant that just as truly as when He was begotten of the Father, He received divine life and glory from Him. Thus the continuation of that life came only by an eternal process of giving and receiving, as absolute as is the eternal generation itself. The more closely we study this truth and Christ's life in the light of it, the more we are compelled to say, that the deepest root of Christ's relationship to the Father, the secret of His glorifying the Father, was this: *He allowed God to do all in Him*. He only received and worked out what God worked in Him. His whole attitude was that of the open ear, the servant spirit, and the childlike dependence that waited for all on God.

Christ Gives His Life To Us

The infinite importance of this truth in the Christian life is easily felt. The life Christ lived in the Father is the life He imparts to us. We are to abide in Him and He in us, *even as* He in the Father and the Father in Him. If the secret of His abiding in the Father is this unceasing self-

170

denial—"I can do nothing of Myself"—this life of most entire and absolute dependence and waiting upon God should be the most marked feature of our Christian life. It must be the first and all-pervading disposition we seek to maintain.

In a book by William Law, he especially insists upon this in his striking repetition of the call. We must die to self in order to have the birth of divine love in our souls. We must sink down in humility, meekness, patience, and resignation to God. I think that all who enter into this advice will feel the new point given by remembering how this entire self-renunciation was not only one of the many virtues in the character of Christ, but the first essential one. Without this self-denial, God could have worked nothing in Him; through this self-denial God worked all.

Let us make Christ's words our own. *"I can do nothing of Myself."* Take it as the keynote of a single day. Look up and see the infinite God waiting to do everything as soon as we are ready to give up all to Him and receive all from Him. Bow down in humble worship and wait for the Holy Spirit to work some measure of the mind of Christ in you. Do not be disconcerted if you do not learn the lesson at once. There is the God of love waiting to do everything in him who is willing to be nothing. At moments the teaching appears dangerous, at other times terribly difficult. The Blessed Son of God teaches it to us. This was His whole life. I can do nothing of Myself. He is our life. He will work it in us. And, when, as the Lamb of God,

He begets His disposition in us, we will be prepared for Him to shine in us in His heavenly glory.

"Nothing of Myself"—that word spoken nearly two thousand years ago, coming out of the inmost depths of the heart of the Son of God—is a seed in which the power of the eternal life is hidden. Take it straight from the heart of Christ and hide it in your heart. Meditate on it until it reveals the beauty of His divine meekness and humility and explains how all the power and glory of God could work in Him. Believe in it as containing the very life and disposition which you need. Believe in Christ whose Spirit dwells in the seed to make it true in you.

Begin in single acts of self-emptying to offer it to God as the one desire of your heart. Count upon God accepting them and meeting them with His grace to make the acts into habits and the habits into dispositions. And, you can depend on it. There is nothing that will lift you so near to God, nothing that will unite you closer to Christ, nothing that will prepare you for the abiding presence and power of God working in you, as the death to self which is found in the simple words—Nothing of Myself.

This word is one of the keys to the New Covenant life. As I believe that God is actually to work all in me, I will see that the one thing that is hindering me is my doing something of myself. As I am willing to learn from Christ by the Holy Spirit to say truly, *Nothing of myself*, I will have the true preparation to receive all God has engaged to work and the power to confidently expect it. I will learn that the whole secret of the New Covenant is just one thing, *God works all!* The seal of the Covenant stands sure. "I the Lord have spoken it, and will do it" (Ezekiel 22:14).